Praise for Vivien Goldman's *Reveng*

"Revelatory . . . feels like an exhilarating conversation with the coolest aunt you never had, as she leaps from one passion to the next."
—*Rolling Stone*

"It doesn't just retell the story of punk with an added woman or two; it centers the relationships between gender and the genre, showing how, through the right lens, the story of punk is a story about women's ingenuity and power."—NPR

"An engaging and politically charged exploration of women in music looking to the past, present, and future."—*Bust Magazine*

"The music journalist and professor combines her academic prowess with the passion she absorbed as an original she-punk herself, magnifying how deeply embedded women's narratives of self-discovery and empowerment are within the history of punk."
—*Wall Street Journal Magazine*

"The language is urgent, often furious, sometimes funny and full of piquant turns of phrase . . . her understanding is wide-ranging and determinedly global, traveling way beyond the old DIY clichés."
—Fiona Sturges, *The Guardian*

"A spirited counter-argument to the male-centric narrative of punk rock . . . she captures the artists and their music with sharply focused eyes and ears and a capacious mind. The book, like the music it deals with, is gutsy, bracing, blunt, and sometimes fun. An essential primer."
—*The Nation*

"While Goldman jumps around, hopping from band to band, she places the female musical foment within the critical context of feminist theory and the cultural context of society's upheaval . . . Known as the 'Punk Professor' as an adjunct at NYU, Goldman extends her authority here."—*Kirkus*

"With her visceral style, Goldman blends interviews, history, and her personal experience as one of Britain's first female music writers in a book that reads like a vivid documentary of a genre defined by dismantling boundaries."—Rough Trade, "Books of the Year 2019"

ALSO BY VIVIEN GOLDMAN

BOOKS

The Book of Exodus: The Making and Meaning of Bob Marley and the Wailers' Album of the Century (2006)

The Black Chord—Visions of the Groove: Connections between Afro-Beats, Rhythm and Blues, Hip Hop, and More, with photographer David Corio (1999)

Pearl's Delicious Jamaican Dishes: Recipes from Pearl Bell's Repertoire (1992)

Kid Creole and the Coconuts: Indiscreet (1984)

Bob Marley: Soul Rebel—Natural Mystic, with photographer Adrian Boot (1981)

MUSIC

Resolutionary (Songs 1979–1982) (2016)

It's Only Money, Chantage, with Eve Blouin (1983)

Dirty Washing (1981)

The Flying Lizards (1980)

REVENGE OF THE SHE-PUNKS

A FEMINIST MUSIC HISTORY FROM POLY STYRENE TO PUSSY RIOT

Vivien Goldman

UNIVERSITY OF TEXAS PRESS ❤ AUSTIN

Cover and interior design by Amanda Weiss

Requests for permission to reproduce material
from this work should be sent to:

PERMISSIONS
University of Texas Press
P.O. Box 7819
Austin, TX 78713-7819
utpress.utexas.edu/rp-form

♾ The paper used in this book meets the minimum requirements of ANSI/
NISO Z39.48-1992 (R1997) (Permanence of Paper).

LIBRARY OF CONGRESS CATALOGING-IN-PUBLICATION DATA
Names: Goldman, Vivien, author.
Title: Revenge of the she-punks : a feminist music history
from Poly Styrene to Pussy Riot / Vivien Goldman.
Description: First edition. | Austin : University of Texas Press,
2019. | Includes index.
Identifiers: LCCN 2018044437
ISBN 978-1-4773-1654-2 (pbk : alk. paper)
ISBN 978-1-4773-1845-4 (library e-book)
ISBN 978-1-4773-1846-1 (non-library e-book)
Subjects: LCSH: Punk rock music—History and criticism. | Feminism
and music. | Women punk rock musicians. | Punk rock musicians.
Classification: LCC ML82 .G64 2019 | DDC 781.66082—DC23
LC record available at https://lccn.loc.gov/2018044437

DOI:10.7560/316542

CONTENTS

WOMANIFESTO

The Opening Vamp

Suddenly there seem to be an awful lot of women musicians, or women bands, in the *Sounds* gig guide. It seems that a women's underground is suddenly emerging overground. . . . When women perform a professional, hard-rocking set, with no concession to female stereotypes, they're an automatic threat. They're a threat to men because they challenge male supremacy in a citadel that has never been attacked before; they threaten women who perhaps never dared acknowledge that THEY want to be onstage doing the energizing instead of watching their boyfriends do it, in passive admiration.

Vivien Goldman, *Sounds*, December 11, 1976

Where are you going? Where have you been?

Jayne Cortez, "Maintain Control," 1986

It all began with glitter. My love of glitter started even before David Bowie, shaking those clear amber plastic maracas seamed with flecks of gold in a percussion dance set named after the bandleader, Victor Silvester. The scene is set in North West London, early 1960s. My father, Max, plays his violin; big sister, Judy, is on keyboards, that is, our piano; myself and middle sister, Susan, hold down the percussion and sing. All three of us girls do. Judy now says I had it easy because I was the youngest and she fought the battles to stay out late. But looking back, I feel like I was always the one being told what to do—except for when we were singing. Then, it was understood that I was the one who heard the harmonies and could tell them the notes.

Music has been my dance partner through life. Merrily, melodramatically, we have waltzed through a whirl of personae: (briefly) press officer, journalist, author, songwriter, singer, producer, club-runner, documentarian, blogger, editor, video/TV/radio writer, director, host and producer, publisher.

My numerous adventures were all instructive. Talked into it against my better judgement, I dabbled in management (very briefly) steering the mid-1970s careers of Generation X (hello, Billy Idol and Tony James!) and the girl duo Snatch, whose Patti Palladin and Judy Nylon cut the plea of the frustrated female artist: "All I want is all you know." When I dropped out of recording (about which there's more anon), I went into independent television as a producer and director in the early 1980s boom. I got to mix up international music on the TV show I devised with a partner, "Big World Café." Videos I directed for to-be-classics back then are in museums today, like rappers Eric B & Rakim's "I Ain't No Joke" and Jamaica's Chaka Demus & Pliers' "Murder She Wrote." Because of music, I stood alone before the guns of a secret army division in Lagos, Nigeria. Once I carried on dancing as bullets flew around me in a Jamaican DJ session because I thought the sounds were the current synth drum beat and the people crouching around me were doing the "Get Flat" dance craze. Afterwards, I was baffled when people congratulated my courage. Eventually, I earned the *nom d'academe* the Punk Professor as a long-serving Adjunct Professor at NYU's Tisch School of the Arts Clive Davis Institute of Recorded Music.

* * *

But the trip to writing this book really began in 1975, writing the above article on women in rock for *Sounds*, the feisty underdog punk rock weekly I had just joined as a writer. By the 1990s that angle had become a predictable annual staple of rock magazines, especially those that rarely covered freethinking She-Punks. But back then, I had never seen such a piece, nor indeed such women. Puzzlement was my overriding feeling as I pushed my way nearer to the front of the London club stage. I was a recent graduate from Warwick, one of Britain's radical new "plateglass" universities. The noted feminist theorist Germaine Greer was my tutor. She disapproved of my partying all term and cramming my studies at exam time. But what did she expect? We loved making music, but I had rarely raved, coming from my rather orthodox Jewish family. The first girl to go to university, I also seemed to be the only one not to want marriage to be my next step in the dance. Instead, I was consumed with a raging curiosity: What could possibly be out there for a weirdo like me? There were no examples, no mentors to look to or advise me.

And now here I was witnessing this strange apparition . . . a long-haired guitarist in jeans, who as I drew closer I realized was—a woman! Playing power chords! I had never seen a girl play on stage in a band before. The shock was such that I had to talk about it with my colleagues at *Sounds*. And so I published my first "Women in Rock" story, which, as you can see, would not be my last. Pop and rock had only really existed for a quarter century, thus making it easy to become an expert. It would have been hard then to imagine that I would turn out to be a music lifer.

Despite its punk identification, *Sounds* was typical of the world of work in the London music industry. Even when I had wo/manhandled my way to features editor, conducting editorial meetings meant dodging a barrage of attempted gender/career genocide—"my" writers, all white and all boys, insisted: "Women don't buy music!" "Women don't make music!" "Women don't read music papers!" The subtext was: "Even if they happen to, they're so irrelevant that why bother to write about them?"

They had all internalized diarist Samuel Johnson's sick eighteenth-century quip: "A woman's preaching is like a dog's walking on his hind legs. It is not done well; but you are surprised to find it done at all." It was natural to bitch about this silliness as I was still having to deal with it, two hundred years on. They were my writers, my team, but those patronizing attitudes also made them my gender enemy. So, what am I then, chopped vinyl? I fumed, often aloud but not always, as I had a weekly paper to fill. An important caveat: not all my male cohorts were in that camp. Just lots of them. The cool ones are still my friends. And I did find a wo/mentor in activist artist Caroline Coon, who also covered punk. Equally, I did get to interview some outstanding women pre-She-Punk, notably the supremely gracious Gladys Knight; super-fun Stevie Nicks of Fleetwood Mac, whom I took shopping in Portobello Road market under the iconic Westway, where she loaded up on vintage gear; operatic Diamanda Galas, whose thrilling, terrifying dual-voiced overtone vocal skills shattered glass ceilings, presaging the work of Canadian Inuit singer-songwriter Tanya Tagaq a half century on; and avant-garde keyboard player Annette Peacock. She lived with her daughter in a squat near me behind Holland Park in Frestonia, the prototypical free state within London, in the kind of libertarian micro-utopia envisioned in the classic British film *Passport to Pimlico*. (Squats will loom large in this saga, wherever She-Punks find themselves.) Again, decades on, cult shero Peacock would inspire Russia's Nastya Mineralova, a music-maker in the activist Pussy Riot collective.

Did sheer cussedness dictate that I would still be writing about women making fascinating music almost fifty years on? No, or not that alone. I want to share the wonder and sheer exultation of recognition that filled me when I first heard Poly Styrene of X-Ray Spex shout, "Oh Bondage, Up Yours!" In those more vanilla days, I knew at once that with all its saucy frisson, the bondage she sang about was not S&M; rather, it was the patriarchy I had been hearing about since feminism had started to filter through just a few years before. In her black garbage bag frock and with a colander for a hat, Styrene was an unprecedented apparition of liberation. She was shouting that I could be part of a community of creative musical girls, probably for the first time since I arranged my two big sisters' harmonies.

But where were the rest of the women? Simple: at that particular moment when punk first stirred, in our pop world, there kinda weren't any, barring the dear presences of Olivia Newton-John, ABBA, and Boney M. It took a few years for outfits like Prince and the Revolution and Kid Creole and the Coconuts to embrace girls in their lineups. Rock trotted along its set boys-own courses, drunk on its lighting, mega stage sets, and big willy speakers, getting hard when the volume went up to eleven and a half.

The best-advertised function for women in 1960s rock was being a groupie—a chick whose validation and self-worth came from snagging and shagging rock stars, the bigger the better. More than an erotic choice, groupiedom was a diversionary displacement, a surrogate for being a rock star onself, which seemed an impossibility. Although groupies did look like rock stars, often better, that job description was not for girls. Respect to the few bold exceptions, like proto-punk Genya Ravan's 1960s group Goldie and the Gingerbreads; the Millington sisters of early 1970s rockers Fanny; and the Wilson sisters of their Canadian contemporaries, Heart. But generally, pre-punk, the more closely a female artist physically resembled Joni Mitchell—tall, thin, and Aryan—the better. She pushed it to sophisticated heights, and vibrant female folkies like Sandy Denny and Maddy Prior could reenvision the light and dark of our ancient canon and make it sing differently for fresh generations. But within the pop pantheon, folk was the approved slot for girls. Prototypical black-leathered girl rocker Suzi Quatro agreed with the door policy, so she was let in. For Quatro, it was enough to get in to the party; she wasn't trying to change what was on the record player. Artists like the world's first black punk, the mixed-race Poly Styrene with frizzy hair and braces, would likely have been deemed unfuckable, thus unmarketable, by the old-school record industry. Yet with her ear for a hook, incisive wit, and expansive political and spiritual consciousness, she immediately became one of punk's great sheroes, her unfettered howl shattering the idea that girls had to sing prettily to be heard.

Everything changed, quite suddenly, when punk kicked off. Instead of *Sounds'* usual seemly exchanges with multinational record companies such as Polydor and EMI, and their well-tested icons—1960s superstars like Rod Stewart, Elton John, the Who, and Pink Floyd were our prey at editorial meetings, access dueled over with rival papers—this hitherto unknown, scruffy, xeroxed, *unofficial* lot were storming our office and our awareness. It was a proper counterculture in action, injecting unpredictable fizz into a stale scene. Punk was a music for and by outsiders, and technical virtuosity was irrelevant; absolute beginners were almost preferred. We had the swiftly ascendant male figureheads of punk like the Sex Pistols and the Clash, easily slotted into a line of descent from the Beatles and the Rolling Stones. But under punk's inclusionary cover, all sorts of oddballs were smuggling themselves past the cock-rock guards—even women!

Of course, there had been women's music scenes in the past. Raunchy female blues singers of the 1920s strutted their individuality, but outside of, say, the lesbian feminist labels of the West Coast 1970s, few women could control their means of production as much as the first indie She-Punks, ensuring an uncut creation.

Equally suddenly, as my article of the time says, individual girls were playing in groups, like bassie (bass player) Gaye Advert in the Adverts. Siouxsie Sioux of Siouxsie and the Banshees was such a dominant presence that she overshadowed the boys in the band— and they knew they were lucky to have her. The first wave of She-Punks—those I met in London like the Slits, the Raincoats, the Mo-Dettes, the Au Pairs, the Passions, and the Delta 5, plus those I just heard, like Germany's Malaria!, Switzerland's Kleenex, or Paris's Lizzy Mercier Descloux—lifted me up and carried me, whooping, body-surfing punk's crest above a macho mosh pit.

In New York, I came to know my labelmates on 99 Records, including ESG, denizens of the Bronx projects who injected funk into punk, and the icebox Bush Tetras. Patti Smith told me how it felt to fall off the stage at a show—and get back up to keep on performing. Knowing and working with them all would forever shape my understanding and creativity, giving me confidence and even hope. Seeing, hearing their work echo down the decades in a loop that seems set to be infinite is encouraging, even exhilarating.

Our story has deep roots. 'Twas likely revenge against those who would send her to debtor's prison that drove, say, Aphra Behn, the sole known female Restoration playwright, author of *Abdelazer, or, The Moor's Revenge* (1676), to muscle her work onstage when Revenge dramas were all the rage but girl playwrights weren't.

So this book is an attempt at a healing . . . and yes, even a noncorrosive revenge, as the title suggests. "I don't *do* revenge," drawled Chrissie Hynde on hearing the title. Yes, but we're not talking that mean-spirited sort of *gotcha!* revenge. In the case of punky females, revenge means getting the same access as your male peers, to make your own music, look and sound how you want, and be able to draw enough people to ensure the continuation of the process. Sounds simple enough, talent permitting, but as this book shows, it's different for girls. In her *We Should All Be Feminists*, Chimamanda Ngozi Adichie writes, "Of course I am a human being, but there are particular things that happen to me because I am a woman." Our path is beset with particular pitfalls, which makes our glories all the sweeter.

Shortly before punk, a feminist work by Tillie Olsen, *Silences*, chronicled the culturally or institutionally enforced silences of the less franchised. She spoke of books, but her observations apply equally to music. After noting how few black writers of the time had been able to get more than one book published, she continued to identify affected sectors of society, including: "those whose waking hours are all struggle for existence; the barely educated; the illiterate; women. Their silence the silence of centuries."

Such imposed lacunae are a pattern of this book and women's history in general. Thus, *revenge* here means assembling at least some voices of various waves of women's punk from disparate communities and considering their differences and connections. To date, the ebb of influence has been largely one-way, from rich world to poor—though that may change. Our revenge is our complex survival.

In a rather punk approach, She-Punks have lurched forward in a series of Year Zeroes, often building on neither the more conventional rock foundation supplied by African American blues nor their own womanly legacy.

Thus, when the estrogen attitude of mid-1970s British girly punk was revived in a more organized, activist form in America's Riot Grrrl movement a decade-plus on, we thought the contribution of first wavers was virtually unknown. Outside of Kurt Cobain of Nirvana championing the Raincoats, we felt forgotten—but research in this book proves our sound had carried rather further than we thought.

Plus, by definition pop is a fickle, forgetful medium. Even before the twenty-first century's online tsunami of musical information, musicians were regularly forgotten after grabbing their moment in fame's quickly pivoting spotlight. Until quite recently, it seemed that after first-wave punk many of our female artists were lost to pop's collective amnesia, even more thoroughly than their boy counterparts. This was brought home to me when Melissa Logan and Alex Murray-Leslie of the vibrant art/music collective Chicks on Speed tracked me down (pre-internet), saying that they had been trying to discover and construct a women's musical lineage, and it had not been easy. Their influential *Girl Monster* compilation, curated by Murray-Leslie, included my own "Launderette."

Writing from the University of Technology in Sydney, Australia, where she is researching computer-enhanced wearable musical instruments, Murray-Leslie remembers, "I'd found a treasure chest of women's music that had been hidden from me in culture, in art/music history lessons at school, and I wanted everyone to hear our voices. . . . especially younger women, so they wouldn't think there's no herstory, they have someone to look, to learn from and a legacy to build on—we're all links in a long strong chain."

That shared attitude animates this book. The leap that Chicks on Speed took when they called me—I had not heard of them—is the sort of rope bridge that my artist sisterwomen and I have repeatedly had to sling over the chasm of deliberate cultural erasure. Hopefully this book will give us one solid step more.

Nonetheless, pop also loves to eat itself, and finally it got around to eating me. When I first wrote about popular music, its history was brief. But since then, it has proliferated wildly and widely, and, like fashion, pop found that it needs to regularly rehydrate at the well of its origins. During the early 1980s, I had crossed the line from writing to composing and singing and had been lucky enough to make music with top people like the Flying Lizards, Public Image Limited, dubmaster Adrian Sherwood, the Raincoats and the Slits, and my partner in the French duo Chantage, Eve Blouin. And so I, too, was rediscovered. Around the time that my few scattered songs were being pulled into the *Resolutionary* album by a European indie label, I noticed that more attention was starting to be paid to my fellow female punks and post-punks. An influential double reissue compilation called *Sharon Signs to Cherry Red* gathered music from a swathe of girl bands. Widely lauded, it was a timely reminder of the breadth of music that these often-forgotten girls had made, and a reminder of how much more difficult it was for the girls to sustain a career because of issues ranging from restrictions by the aforesaid cock-rock contingent to the difficulty of regular childcare for a single mother.

Pitchfork magazine ran a women's feminist punk piece in 2016, to which I contributed. It was another nudge. Punk really did blast open a cultural space for women's musical community, in a literally unprecedented way. By studying, listening to, and grooving with these She-Punks' work, made over decades and around the world, I hope to divine our shared concerns. What drives the fierce femmes of this ongoing musical revolution? I hope you will find an answer in these pages.

Although this one volume cannot be seen as definitive, it does represent an initial attempt to open up the dialog about female punk's international impact. By including artists from beyond the better-known spheres of the United Kingdom and United States, I hope to show how and why the seismic aftershocks of punk's beginnings in volatile but super-creative 1970s Britain went on to shake up women everywhere.

Is conflict, in fact, a necessary step in a girl punk's path? Maybe not today, when some argue that punk's rebel spirit is defanged, having been co-opted by the British government (disclosure: I too have sucked on that nipple, believing that spreading the rebel punk word validated the ironic establishment embrace). Now hip parents buy their girls guitars and encourage tattoos and hair experiments that would once have prompted lockdowns.

* * *

That female artists around the world, almost half a century after the movement was born, still choose to present as punk might have been a surprise in its scrappy nights of origin. Subculture mavens often aim to claim the genre as their own, pertaining to, say, the few square miles around the storied CBGB club on New York's then-gritty, now-posh Bowery, or equally to the streets around London's Westway, where punk and reggae first coalesced for me and my crew. Certainly, the birth of punk nation is eagerly claimed by various factions. (I like to point out its little-sung roots in Paris, France.) But hopefully, the diversity of these She-Punks proves that punk belongs to everyone.

If in doubt, look to Manila in the Philippines, whose lively music scene has been female friendly since the 1980s. Their all-girl feminist punk band the Male Gaze was co-founded by fashion designer/musician Mich Dulce in 2017, after meeting like-minded guitarist Mariah Reodica at a collective Dulce had begun, a safe space for women that she called Grrrl Gang Manila; their peppy power-punk was inspired by original American Riot Grrrl bands like Bikini Kill and Le Tigre. "We wanted a feminist rather than just an all-girl band, one which really had a clear messaging for gender equality and women's rights. Our president Duterte is churning out misogynist statements promoting gender-based violence on a daily basis. We felt it was important to use our music as a tool to counter his statements," Dulce says.

How natural that the Filipina musicians should choose punk, out of all the genres available, as their confrontational form of expression. As the primal yowl of a rebellious underclass, punk has always specially belonged to girls. For this writer, punk's most enduring and significant achievement will always be its liberating impact on the less-privileged sex. But let's not kid ourselves. It may have been a bit friendlier in the Philippines, but virtually all these She-Punks' breakthroughs have been in spite of gender-specific struggles; and although we live in a time where some of the music industry's biggest earners are female artists, it does not mean that She-Punks are not among the severely challenged. Women still have no controlling say in the multinational music industry for which we earn so much. Within show business, we are often regarded as replaceable fresh meat, best consumed when young. That's why punk is so great for girls—it allows or even encourages the artist to roar the anger that always pumps beneath the style's skin—and our own.

And we still have reason to roar. With chilling synchronicity, while this book was being written in America, threats were being made at the highest governmental level to decimate basic women's rights that we had come to take for granted, attacks on our individual autonomy and civil liberties that we had assumed were firmly established (in the rich world, at least) more or less since the 1960s.

* * *

A spotlight suddenly swung on the toxic everyday harassment of women by cultural gatekeeper males in the entertainment business, which my girlfriends and I had grown accustomed to battling for decades. Establishment heroes from Bill Cosby to Harvey Weinstein, even music industry figures like much-loved hip-hop producer/yoga guru Russell Simmons, began toppling like statues of Confederate generals in the South. Rumors of a backlash began almost immediately, to no one's surprise. While the shape of our hopefully fairer future leadership comes into focus, the witch, Amazon, or Valkyrie within us all is being called back to the barricades. She-Punks have been singing about these issues since the style began—and still do.

And there are always more paths to trace, to sing about. Activism and womanist pride and defiance are rising, and debates include the meaning or essence of womanhood; as I was delivering this book, the *Guardian* reported that a transgender woman had breastfed her own baby for the first time in human existence. Arguably more people than ever, these artists among them, have been testing the fluid, porous possibilities of gender. The impact of such developments on the future of women's music—where, why, and how it is made, performed, marketed, distributed, and sold—remains to be sung. In this state of flux, boundaries are swiftly sketched and redrawn, as young activist musician and Londoner Tyson McVey discovered when she and some girlfriends started a party/discussion night, the Ladies' Music Pub, in 2013. The chatty handle soon became a target. "Things change so fast. At first, people wanted us to change our name because they weren't sure about feminism—and now we get criticized because transgender or nonbinary people sometimes feel excluded by the word *ladies*," McVey explains. "Technology and online activism keep pushing the debate forward. It can be frustrating, because it sometimes feels like there is so much you can't say or do. But it is an interesting time."

From such tumultuous debates, new possibilities emerge. Increasingly, musicians face the need for autonomy, independence, and personal responsibility, for a 360-degree understanding of not only their art, but how to get it heard in such a way that they can continue to make more, as and when they desire. Reading the tea leaves of experience, this bodes well for female artists, who are often used to functioning outside the old-school boys-own industry mainstream, as these pages show.

* * *

Will the arguments ever end? Hopefully not. How much more binary, restricted, and less diverse was the night when I saw that lone, unknown girl guitarist jamming in the mid-1970s? Thrashing her unicorn's mane, she lit an urge within. I wondered, How did she get there? And how will she keep working as a musician when no other girl has done it, except for the outliers' outliers, Motown session bass player Carol Kaye and the glamorous beehived Lady Bo (Peggy Malone, née Jones), whose chicken scratch rhythm guitar helped Bo Diddley be a gunslinger? (No doubt it also underlined how my potential path was as big a mystery.) I am still wondering, so I wrote this book. Putting together the experiences of these female punks and their foremothers was, even for me who had helped lay some trails, a sort of mapmaking into unknown territory.

Striking off the familiar path to slash out a route for *Revenge of the She-Punks*, I set my compass by songs around themes, presented in each chapter's introductory playlist, instead of linear chronology. Each leg of the journey is signposted by, structured around, the playlists' individual tracks. By pursuing the fundamental common concerns—identity, money, an emotional life, making change—that these very different international female musicians have recorded about since punk began, my thought is that routes to fully realizing our creative futures will become clearer. In order to realize this, in addition to a lifetime in the punkette trenches, I spent two years tracking down and interviewing these forty-three internationally based artists, and more. So, hopefully, this is the book that would have done me good when I was wondering how I would ever be able to find my own way.

Some women herein are semi-separatist. Some insist on being in a mixed-gender group, or the sole girl in a band of boys. Yet one thing is sure. There is strength when we huddle around the (metaphorical) fire as women together—with backing vocals from the men who love us—to dance, sing, and share our stories and our songs.

So, who is going to start?

LINEUP & TRACK LISTING:

1. Poly Styrene/X-Ray Spex, "Identity" (UK, 1976).
The singer of X-Ray Spex, Poly Styrene, was an ecstatic, visionary Anglo-Somalian punk godmother. Here, her inimitable expression points to what would grow to become an increasingly dominant discussion.

2. Blondie, "Rip Her to Shreds" (US, 1977).
Versatile Debbie Harry becomes New Wave diva as Blondie with compadre guitarist Chris Stein.

3. The Raincoats, "No One's Little Girl" (UK, 1983).
Setting a template for experimental feminist post-punk.

4. Kathleen Hanna/Bikini Kill, "Rebel Girl" (US, 1993).
Creating the global Riot Grrrl movement and unleashing a torrent of girl pain, eased by punk.

5. Lizzy Mercier Descloux/Rosa Yemen, "Rosa Vertov" (France, 1979).
Vagabond Parisian poet, painter, and punkette explores her voice.

6. Tamar-kali, "Pearl" (US, 2014).
The Geechee Goddess of Afro-Punk relates punk to the independence of her Gullah ancestry.

7. Big Joanie, "Dream Number 9" (UK, 2016).
Electro funk-punk from South London activist artists.

8. Delta 5, "Mind Your Own Business" (UK, 1979).
Agit-funk from the Leftist Leeds school of angular post-punk.

9. Bush Tetras, "Too Many Creeps" (US, 1983).
Aggravation from dickhead/doofus nation annoys these arbiters of New York's No Wave downtown deadpan cool.

10. Fea, "Mujer Moderna" ("Modern Woman") (US, 2016).
Texan Chicana punks assert their rights in a traditional culture.

1

GIRLY IDENTITY

Who Be Me?

We realize that the only people who care enough about us to work consistently for our liberation are us. Our politics evolve from a healthy love for ourselves, our sisters and our community which allows us to continue our struggle and work. This focusing upon our own oppression is embodied in the concept of identity politics.

Combahee River Collective Statement, 1977

What is this women's music? I haven't heard enough of it, sadly, to be able to lay many handy guidelines, but it might have something to do with the way the Raincoats organize themselves and their instruments, no lead singers or players, a conscious change from the top-dog/underdog pattern set up by the patriarchal structure.

Vivien Goldman, *Melody Maker*, December 1, 1979

TOO OBSESSIVE A QUEST for identity can result in people quite forgetting who they are. Among punk's great liberators was its encouragement to rename and re-place oneself and not be saddled with ancestral sagas. But a bright inner pulse pushes us to understand where, how, and why we fit into this increasingly fractured world, to seek a space where even committed non-belongers might belong. This lure is a twinkling trickster pulling us into deep psychic forests where analysts cannot follow.

We first-generation Brit punkettes stumbled through dark trees whose big, twisted roots could trip us up—the competing needs of our womanhood and desire to make something of our own happen, versus the unthinkable-or-else-they-would-be-insurmountable odds stacked like logs on a witch-burning pyre to burn our autonomy to ashes. Institutionally and intellectually, new ideas were outshining them to light the path out—volleys of hot conceptual bullets shot by illuminated minds like Kate Millett, Maya Angelou, and Gloria Steinem, and the collective writings of America's *Ms* magazine in 1972, followed the next year by Britain's *Spare Rib*. Fire to fight fire—but how would our musical blaze sound?

There were no role models, or barely, outside of certain twentieth-century jazz and blues singers and their ilk. With the rising interest in spectacular foremothers, their glorious but embattled lives spent trying to carve out their own space to create among all that dense dickwood, would be commemorated in documentaries and biopics: Nina Simone, Bessie Smith, Billie Holiday. After all, it was a white male monopoly that banned Holiday from singing in public by taking away her cabaret license in 1947. Trapped by history, race, gender, and class, she was one of those who paid the heaviest price.

All these punk women, however, had more space to try identities on for size till they found the right fit. As my quote from a 1979 Raincoats interview asks, What sound would we make, now that we finally could? Who were we, newly emboldened to think that our basic women's rights would henceforth roll down like rain; and who were we going to be, now that we could try on a new identity like a new hat and brave the consequences? And would the hat cost what it said on the tag? In so many ways, women had been paying the price of systemic powerlessness, domestically disenfranchised, publicly and professionally mocked, or rendered invisible. One way or the other, en route to the bright future, as usual, women were bound to bleed.

The sacrificial scourges of early-twenty-first-century girls, words like *bulimia, anorexia,* and *cutting,* were almost unknown in Britain in the early 1970s. Though all three demons existed, there was no name to be whispered in changing-rooms or kitchens about such self-mutilating horrors. Yet seeing physical self-harm happen, a cutting that could have led to death right there in the ladies' room, drove a questing, imaginative British teenager called Marianne Joan Elliott-Said to go home and write in her diary. The grisly incident became part of her process of using art to try and understand herself and her place in society. The new freedom of punk gave her the creative space to do it in music as well as pages she thought only she would see. Thus wrote Poly Styrene of X-Ray Spex in her diary when she got home: "Tracy a sales assistant from Seditionaries crouches on the floor in a corner of the ladies' powder room scratching, slashing her wrists with a razor. . . ."

"This was one of the inspirations behind the song 'Identity,'" her daughter, Celeste Bell, said.

> The other was of course my mother's struggle with her own sense of identity, growing up as a mixed-race child; first in a very white middle class suburb as a small child and later in a mixed white working class/Afro-Caribbean neighborhood of Brixton. My mother was neither white nor Jamaican (her father was Somalian) and never really felt like she belonged anywhere. Another inspiration behind the song was the tribalism of British youth culture—punks, hippies, Rastas, skins, disco dollies, etc. Everyone was trying to assert their identity via the clothes they wore, the music they listened to, etc. All wanted to be individuals, but they ended up being [just like] everyone else in their own little group.

Countercultural conformity has been skewered before, particularly deliciously in British comedian Tony Hancock's 1961 film

The Rebel, in which he plays a London artist whose giddy daubs (that oddly presage the works of Jean-Michel Basquiat), which he dubs the "shapist school" of art, are taken up by hip Parisian beatniks. They listen, rapt, as he describes the suburban and professional tedium he had escaped, with everybody thinking and dressing alike. The beatniks shudder: what a hideous fate. Of course, all the boys are bearded and the various genders uniformly wear black. But since identity politics was born, just pre-punk, the intent quest for self has been central to women's thinking. Roles hurtle towards us and we try to jet past hurdles as we blaze erratic trails towards elusive yet consistent goals: solidly owning control of our bodies, our homes, our children; our art, our passions, our safety. We can never relax, even when some of these rights seem in our grasp. Our individual issues are the fulcrum of a tug of war among ideologies, values, and beliefs, and all these artists had to thrash out new ways of living, in a break from their foremothers'. Our previously unique right to childbearing has been diffused by technology in the rich world, even as it has made possible new ways of being a family. Over the coming decades, identity studies would experience kudzu-like growth, sometimes threatening to obliterate the imperative to understand oneself as an individual, independent of one's history in the tabula rasa spirit of punk, rather than let history wholly define you. The balance is delicate, as knowing the rhythms of generations of battles helps to prepare one for the next round. But when Poly Styrene sang these words, the whole idea of addressing identity was still novel, let alone in pop:

Identity
Is the crisis
Can't you see
When you look in the mirror
Do you see yourself
On the TV screen

The honking saxophone riff of X-Ray Spex was unusual for punk, and the rhythm is an adrenaline shot. But it was the Klaxon voice of Styrene, in tune but ready to jump off, that grabbed and shook you. With her rampant curls, braces, and (genius) goofy style, Styrene would previously have been an unlikely candidate for pop stardom; but now she situated herself as a leader, sonically and conceptually. Visionary in articulating the quest for identity so specifically, she was voicing the angst of her generation and those to come, as she was born at a pivotal time for societal change. Where to fit in? And how to stand out, express the difference you feel inside, the inner nub of knowing that unfurls like a lotus with each experience? Sifting through over four decades of punk made by women, one thing is clear. Unmoored from what had been, from the 1970s to the early twenty-first century, a remarkable number of them were drawn to address the same primal, existential question: Who am I?

We knew it at the time too. In 1976, Slits guitarist Viviane Albertine told me, "All the guys around me were forming bands, and they had heroes to look up to. But I didn't have anyone. I didn't want to look like or be Joni Mitchell. I didn't even want to be Fanny. Then it suddenly occurred to me that I didn't have to have a hero; I could pick up a guitar and just play. It's not so much why I started playing, as why I didn't play before."

No such self-searching or urge for definition beset the boys, it seems. Pondering the Raincoats in 1979, I noted, "When I interview Stevie Nicks, Gladys Knight, or the Raincoats, about 50 percent of the conversation revolves around feelings, emotions. That's roughly 50 percent more than when I'm interviewing men. The reason probably is that while men are trained and socialized to cultivate their aggression, force, and ambition, women are socialized to have easy access to their emotions and encouraged to express them more freely." Four-plus decades on, those differences may be blurry, but their essence still stands. Any changes reflect how the role and status of the sexes have shifted since early feminism, and also how, because of its comparative simplicity, punk became a launchpad for (often unlearned) female self-expression, a powerful vehicle for thoughts uncut by an old-school, patriarchal industry like the music and entertainment business then as now. As power relations are so skewed and the predators so confident, it clearly makes sense for the unconventional female artist to be prepared to go it alone, create her own community, go the indie route, and take the side road to her destination. Although women in the mainstream have always held powerful positions in areas like marketing and public relations, as punk first yowled, and thus prior to the rise of white pop independent labels, virtually no female people had positions as tastemaking gatekeepers or producers who might go to battle for unconventional girls.

Essentially the story has remained the same, though new technologies have helped girls as one decade's folk singer-songwriter with a guitar, hoping for a deal, became another's bedroom hit-maker, like Little Boots and Dua Lipa from the United Kingdom or Princess Nokia from the United States; they were in a position to float their digital music into the universe and find their fan-base via MySpace, Facebook, Bandcamp, or SoundCloud without having to be approved by the guys in the band or the label. Any advantage must be seized; a 2016 list of the world's one hundred top DJs in *DJ* magazine was almost all white and featured just one woman. The following year, a University of Southern California's Annenberg Inclusion Initiative headed by professor Stacy L. Smith surveyed race and gender in the recording industry. Among the six hundred most popular songs released since 2012, it revealed, women had composed a mere 12.3 percent and performed fewer than 25 percent; the ratio of male to female producers was forty-nine to one. "The voices of women are missing from popular music," concluded Professor Smith.

For an original thinker like Styrene, the official industry path proved tortuous. But her effervescent creativity persisted, always thought-forward, wittily tackling issues like automation and ecology before they became mass debates. Styrene, wittily prophetic to the end, in her last LP—*Generation Indigo*, produced by Martin "Youth" Glover of Killing Joke and released shortly before her death in 2011—sang of digital romance prior to it being the default mode.

She was born to be ahead of her time. Only a quarter century had passed since America had lifted the ban on marriage between couples of different melanin pigmentation. Happily, Britain was less sick in that regard, at least; despite its major role in the slave trade, no such apartheid law ever existed there. The *Daily Mail* announced in mid-2014 that one in ten British couples was ethnically mixed and that racism was diminishing because of it. But in the mid-1970s, when Styrene was hitting notes never previously recorded, she was another sort of forerunner, too, literally a pioneer of a future breed representing a bone-deep fusion of Britain and its old colonies that would later be seen as ordinary. Styrene helped pave the way.

As is often the case with single-mother families like Styrene's, the classic narrative of the absentee father is more complex than it appears. Although her father, Osman Mohammed Said, had a wife at home in Somalia, his connection with her mother, Bromley-born Joan Nora Elliott, was genuine. Their relationship foundered because neither wanted to fully take on the other's culture. Joan refused to have her children raised by others in Somalia or, another option, move there herself, adopt Islam, and live in polygamy. Osman would not—could not?—change his traditional ways, despite his affection for her and their children.

Celeste Bell, Styrene's daughter and a musician who often played with her, says, "Osman fundamentally considered western culture to be corrupting. My mother was able to relate to his point of view as she shared many of his personality traits and was also rather disdainful of western culture (having become a Hare Krishna at twenty-four years old). Although my mum had been raised by an English mother in England, she had never felt English and I believe her soul was essentially Somalian." Of course, the irony is that had Styrene indeed moved to Somalia, local expectations would have given her as many challenges as those she faced at home.

Styrene spent time in a psychiatric hospital and experienced cosmic visions that she later subdued with medication. Says Bell, "Like many young people of color, she was misdiagnosed as schizophrenic. But in fact, she suffered from bipolar I disorder. I believe a lot of her mental distress was caused by the feeling of being stuck on a grey damp island surrounded by people who tended to repress their emotions and passions."

So Poly Styrene was perfect for punk, which was all about feeling uncomfortable in and challenging the status quo. Styrene performed for thousands at Rock Against Racism shows in 1978 and 2008—the organization created to combat the increasing influence of the National Front that has sadly proved to be ever relevant. She claimed her space in those first years of ferment, when music aligned with the exhilarating sense of progress. Three years before "Oh Bondage," the 1974 Sex Discrimination Act began protecting working women; in the year of its release, the UN General Assembly declared the first International Women's Day—and female factory workers, mostly Asian, were in the midst of a years-long strike to unionize their workplace, Grunwick a film processing plant in North West London—which helped politicize a generation and galvanize a movement.

Ultimately, the Grunwick strikers lost their jobs and were effectively betrayed by the all-white, all-male unions they had sought to join. Nonetheless, working conditions were improved—and the strikers were our warrior women. Such obstinate muscles were needed to shift the weight of centuries. Postwar, postcolonial British society was being shaken by the vanishing of all the old certainties, whereby a broke aristocratic younger son could go off to "the Colonies"—British Somaliland, for example, home of Styrene's dad, which was more or less ruled by the British until 1960, ping-ponging the Somali people's identity back and forth with the French and Italians.

* * *

Often disrupted by other postcolonial struggles in the 1970s— with frequent IRA bombs, unemployment awaiting the youth, and strikes that plunged the UK into darkness so that homework was done by candlelight, everyone shivered, and garbage piled high in the street—Britain tried to puzzle out its own identity crisis. It was a conflicted nation in transition to a multicultural society. Within the home, many were still slow to emerge from the engrained mindset that a girl's self-respect and success were defined by the wealth and power of the man she trapped—and has that belief ever really gone away?—as if her own existence was but a shadow. According to such thinking, when the husband/son was removed—whether by death or running off with a younger model, or whatever—the woman's own light was extinguished; her power switched off. The shadow fades into invisibility. Only wealth could brighten the situation.

The free-thinking women of punk took a battering ram to those attitudes. But one of first-wave punk's most beloved songs, Blondie's 1977 "Rip Her to Shreds," channeled a veteran sensibility that has never left. The 1950s rockabilly look would not be widely popular again till the '80s revival, and punks of the period liked to remind everyone that "Elvis Is Dead," the old grinder's passing being a fault line between rock and punk's brave new genre. Yet Blondie—the partnership between archetypal blonde Debbie Harry and her partner in music, then life, guitarist Chris Stein—had worldwide success with a tune about very un-punk, rival Mean Girls, before they became a category thanks to comic *auteur* Tina Fey. Harry delivers with juicy '50s girl group relish, well up for a cat fight in a back alley over the captain of the high school football team—and we know who would be homecoming queen. Punk's own Marilyn Monroe, Harry's diamond-faceted cheekbones helped make her punk's big crush and soon a global chart staple. But punk was just another look for Blondie, really. She was a folkie first, in the quaintly named outfit Wind in the Willows. Collaborating with Stein, she worked skillfully in several different genres—effectively absorbing disco in "Heart of Glass" and introducing global dance floors to hip-hop with "Rapture." In her later career, Harry became a jazz singer—while still performing as Blondie. She was authentic in each incarnation. The couple were both musically flexible. As Stein observes, "Blondie thought of ourselves more as a pop than a punk band, but we did operate within the parameters of the form from time to time."

They first played together in the Stilettos, a cabaret/mash-up group; their fellow singers, sisters Tish and Eileen Bellomo, a.k.a. Tish and Snooky, would later color the world punk with an innovative line of lurid hair dyes called Manic Panic.

The Stilettos' tongue-in-cheek retro got restyled for "Rip Her to Shreds," and it was still a good look. Nostalgia often swings in two-decade cycles, making the 1950s just far enough back from the '70s to be exotic and have the allure of a supposedly simpler time (not that it was, in fact). And 1970s artists were often raised by 1950s kids.

"We liked the 1950s, because everything was rawer back then. We were all enamored of girl groups like the Shangri-Las and the Ronettes; they had a punk attitude though they were slicker," recalls Stein. "I didn't get it when I was a little kid; I thought it was commercial. But once I was in my band period, I realized how brilliant and dramatic it was. ["Rip Her to Shreds"] also has a self-deprecating aspect; it is a little self-directed at Debbie, who used to worry about being [seen as] dumb. That is in the mix somewhere," he notes affectionately.

"Debbie always says that the song is a mash-up of a conglomerate of different women that were around and that we ran into. A lot of mind games and one-upmanship went on [in the first NY punk wave], and I can't say for sure that the guys didn't participate in their own way."

Oh, you know her, "Miss Groupie Supreme"
Yeah, you know her, "Vera Vogue" on parade
Yeah, you know her, with the fish-eating grin
She's so dull, come on rip her to shreds

The song was recorded almost live on the first take, with some overdubs, says Stein, concluding, "But people did love that song, right away."

* * *

The polished pastiche un-sisterhood of "Rip Her to Shreds" is the conceptual flip side of the Raincoats' "No One's Little Girl," which is happily shambolic by conventional standards. Opening with soft yelps, the track delights in toying with the voice, sometimes singing in a whisper where the power of volume was always more prized, calling on us to listen differently. The blurry saw of Vicki Aspinall's fiddle enhanced the track's mysterious tug. This faux softness was subversive, undercutting the foundation of people's expectations of how women could or should sound in music. The band illuminated a new register, and a perspective that was defiantly feminist. The New Yorkers of Blondie could be wittily nostalgic for the 1950s while the Raincoats were born to kick against that conformist decade, in which uncomfortable corsets and tight, pointy-toed stiletto heels were not a fun style or even a fetish, but a daily dressing necessity.

"There was definitely a 1950s vibe in my parents' heads," reflected bassist Gina Birch. "My mum was mostly a housewife. She wanted for me the things she knew were good for herself: nice party dresses with silver party shoes, curls though my hair was dead straight, to be girly and dance 'round the living room for aunties to *Swan Lake*. It was secure in its own way. But my mother did not have a lot of friends; she was a bit oppressed, then a bit depressed." Birch and her father were very close, but he disliked her bringing feminist books back from the library, in case they gave her mother ideas. Birch wanted more, though she was not sure what that more could consist of. "Boys were encouraged to be what we would like to be. The life assigned to boys was more adventurous, exciting, and challenging. We girls thought—we would like to have a bit of that!" she recalls. "It's not simple, though, because boys might want to have more enjoyment [of 'womanly' things like] cooking, gardening, nurturing. But it did seem a bigger step for women to find adventures. Then I saw the Slits."

Oral legend was ratified in the script of the insightful, hilarious 2002 Michael Winterbottom film *24 Hour Party People*: only forty-two people saw the Sex Pistols perform their first Manchester show in 1976, "but they all went on to do wondrous things." For Marianne Elliott-Said, seeing the Sex Pistols flipped her previously pop-py artistry; for Gina Birch, seeing the Slits, West London white girls with dreadlocks and perfectly imperfect outfits, perform their off-kilter, dub-infused, reckless music was just such an epiphany. This is what I want to do, she thought. This is it.

"It was as if I was seeing something that I had never seen or entertained before, that had not existed before, not in that way," Birch marvels. "Like getting excited when I discovered conceptual art. The idea of making sculpture out of a piece of marble seemed nothing to do with me. But making a line on a piece of paper with a car wheel like Robert Rauschenberg—that made sense."

Soon, Birch found herself living in a squat off Westbourne Park Road as the bass player of a new band, the Raincoats, fronted by the rasp of their Portuguese singer, Ana da Silva, and including one classically trained member, violinist Vicki Aspinall. As a prototypical post-punk band delighting in unexpected time changes and timbres, the Raincoats were a vital part of the early Rough Trade label's roster. It seemed an auspicious moment, as it had for Poly Styrene. The Raincoats signed in 1977—the year of the first Women's Liberation Movement Conference in London.

The previous year, the Domestic Violence Act had finally legalized a battered woman's right to take out a court order against a violent husband. Women's rights were implicit in the culture of Rough Trade. Set on a run-down street behind Portobello Road, the pioneering independent record store was a nucleus for fanzine makers and DIY musicians, including locals like the Raincoats, the Clash, local reggae band Aswad, and the Slits. Founded on socialist collective lines that Geoff Travis, its founder, had absorbed while working on a kibbutz after high school, the Rough Trade store and subsequent label were ideologically grounded in a bracing gender equality that drew female artists, such as Switzerland's Kleenex, sax player Lora Logic—an alumna of X-Ray Spex—and the Delta 5, as well as the Raincoats.

In this open climate, Birch found her community (including this author) and was empowered to write "No One's Little Girl." She explains her thinking: "Up until I came to London, I was always part of a partnership. I had to have a boyfriend; that was the rule imported from the outside world, which I internalized. Every time I had one, I always entered their zone; they wouldn't enter mine. I would get consumed and lose touch with my girlfriends. Suddenly I realized I didn't need that [validation] and it felt very liberating. I think the song was a 'fuck you' to all that."

> Even if you ask me to
> I'm gonna turn you down
> I won't mess you around
> I'm no one's little girl, oh no, I'm not
> I'm not gonna be—'cause I don't wanna be
>   in your family tree

After the Raincoats played regularly at local West London dives like the Tabernacle and the Acklam Hall, tucked under the concrete arches of the Westway motorway made famous by the Clash, after the frenzy of those few concentrated punk years when we hurled ourselves into freefall and day and night seemed interchangeable in a frenetic forward motion, much changed in London. John Lydon, ex-singer of the Sex Pistols, moved to Los Angeles with his wife, Nora. Her daughter, the Slits' singer Ari Up, went to live in the jungles of Belize with her children. I ventured to Paris and recorded as Chantage with my cosmopolitan music partner, Eve Blouin. The Raincoats, too, took a hiatus in the 1980s, a time of pursuing solo projects including the adoption by Birch and husband Mike of two girls—both of whom grew up to play guitar. Ana da Silva and the band's manager, Shirley McLoughlin, moved to Spain together. Yet the Raincoats were so good at answering that primal question, What might women's music sound like, if it were different from the blokes'? that though they were obscured, they were never forgotten. A decade later, the Raincoats were rediscovered, publicly championed by punk tastemakers including Nirvana's singer-songwriter Kurt Cobain and Sonic Youth's bass player, Kim Gordon. In the next century, they were understood as central to experimental popular music. But it was seeing the Slits that first transformed Birch and her friends, and she never forgot it. "Punk was exciting and it was doable. It enabled a new sensibility to be let loose, unleashed in my heart and brain. I thought, this is the beginning of who I am."

* * *

The reverberations of Gina Birch's buzzing, swooping bass lines in the Raincoats would shake through the decades and resonate across the Atlantic, to America's Northeast in the early 1990s. Caught on bootleg cassettes, they would inspire a multitalented student artist and fashion designer named Kathleen Hanna. Shaken by the rape of her roommate in their own apartment, Hanna decided to extend her creativity into music, specifically to shout about the abhorrent, ill-reported, ill-investigated, and scarily regular abuses of women that were happening around her. Hanna left her emotionally unavailable father, who despised his wife's interest in feminism, to join a creative community centered on liberal arts schools such as Evergreen State College in Olympia, Washington. A go-getter, Hanna, who tells her story affectingly in the documentary *The Punk Singer*, was an instinctive activist and organizer, producing fashion shows of her own designs while in college. Those skills would prove crucial as she helped to seed the political ideas inherent in the Riot Grrrl movement internationally. Music was a medium natural to Hanna, who had both sung and been a spoken word poet in her teens, till the incendiary punk novelist Kathy Acker pointed out to her that music reached more people. Song thus became Hanna's loudspeaker to communicate the abuse of girls and clarify and focus the rage that the issues she sang about with her band, Bikini Kill, should rightly inspire. She has skills like the goddess Kali has arms: creating fanzines, designing flyers, writing slogans that would have made her a fortune in the advertising business. The Raincoats' champion Kurt Cobain composed a global hit based on words that Hanna scrawled in magic marker on his wall for a drunken lark: "Smells Like Teen Spirit." In the 1990s, the writers behind the cunningly faux-feminist Spice Girls plundered Hanna's "Girl Power" slogan. Despite the Spice Girls' being both a manipulated and manipulative construct, Hanna's refracted feminist signals were still picked up by an even wider generation of mostly girl pop pickers.

> That girl thinks she's the queen of the neighborhood
> she holds her head up so high
> I think I want to be her best friend, yeah
> Rebel girl you are the queen of my world . . .
> I want to take you home . . .
> In her kiss, I taste the revolution!

Kathleen Hanna wrote those lyrics at top speed as Bikini Kill rehearsed in a practice space in Washington, DC. Bass player Kathi Wilcox came up with the bass line, and soon the band was playing an energizing, upbeat tune. It flailed and attacked, as punk does, yet it also had a cheeky, almost bubblegum feel. Released in 1993, "Rebel Girl" was unusually exultant and cheering. It soon became definitive, an anthem of ferocious fun for gay and straight girls alike to dance to and feel happy because of its celebration of all forms of positive girl connection.

"It was one of those really weird things, though it sounds super corny," Hanna recalls of that session.

> Like there was something electric in the air and I just tapped into it. I was very close with my friend Laura at the time, having all these conversations. . . . I was pretty stressed out and she helped a lot to keep me together. I wrote it for her, and for me. As I sang it, I remember thinking, "I wish somebody felt this way about me." It was a conglomeration of what was going on then and things from the past. When I was younger, I had been really attracted to a best friend, totally the weirdest person in the whole world. I never told her I wanted to date her; I didn't know [dating girls] was a real thing, it was so not talked about. Nobody around me had any awareness.

"It felt like it wrote itself," she continues.

> I wasn't thinking, "This is an anthem, this is the song that needs to be here now." I am really proud I wrote it from a personal perspective, thinking of the best girlfriends I had had. Girls have angst leveled at them all the time—you're conceited, you're snobby. It's a way to put a tag on your name, ruin your reputation. Thinking of the meanness that girls can do, I wondered—What if instead of saying, "That girl, she thinks she's so great," you could say, "And I think she's so great too. I don't care what you say about her, I'm still going to be her best friend."

As Riot Grrrl grew, spreading through indie 45s, handmade fanzines, and gigs after which bands crashed on fans' floors, Hanna found herself deluged by anguished letters and midnight conversations with young fans; a nonstop torrent of pain, the detritus of tragedies that girls felt emboldened to share through the bravery and artistry of Hanna and her cohorts like Bratmobile, Sleater-Kinney, and L7. Still volunteering as a counselor at a women's crisis center as she had done before the band, Hanna now realized her musical clinic was America, and her client list of girls damaged by rape, incest, school bullying, and violence of unimaginable kinds inflicted almost entirely by males seemed to be infinite.

"I honestly thought men would be psyched that we were breathing life into real issues that affect people. Some guys have been abused. If not, they for sure know someone who is being street harassed. But instead of saying, 'Thanks for educating us, this is awesome,' they hated us instead. It was awful," she laments.

"I went into it much more Pollyanna. I had experienced violence in life but I was very hopeful that this punk scene was about challenging the norms of society. Yet they re-created the same exact abusive family model. Men are taught about power and control and now they often don't have it because of the economy. So they look for a way to get the control they feel they are entitled to and owed. For men of all colors, when they ask, 'What dog do I kick?' the immediate answer often is women and children."

The Riot Grrrls were descendants of early feminist punks, but they built on the foundation laid by bands like the Raincoats. They didn't merely benefit from the ideology; they helped to create one.

"They were more articulate. We were feeble compared to the Riot Grrrls," laughs the Raincoats' Gina Birch. "In the 1970s, women's consciousness-raising groups did not turn into punk bands. Riot Grrrls were more political; we were just fighting for our corner, trying to make sense of our lives rather than attacking the patriarchy." In 1990s England, as Riot Grrrl exploded in

America, it seemed as if the new generation of feminist bands were unaware of the British artists' work; but we were wrong.

Bikini Kill's drummer, Toby Vail, "the most amazing musicologist who never went to school," according to Hanna, had passed cassettes around and hipped both Hanna and her good friend Kurt Cobain onto their elder UK artists like the Raincoats and the Slits. A tape of the latter doing a radio interview left the Americans awed and giggling as the West London wild girls taunted a sleazy interviewer—"I'm waiting for you in the phone box with my raincoat on!" Their very British absurdist humor demolished him—a handy new weapon in the arsenal of the Riot Grrrls. Hanna explains, "It wasn't just like they were girls in a rock band doing it like the guys; it didn't sound the same. They pushed things to another level; they weren't going to play like the guy bands. They schooled us." A reggae fan, Hanna also loved the way both bands incorporated the spaciness and time-warp of dub. After the breakup of Bikini Kill, like any persistent punk whose technique inevitably develops, Hanna's sound developed in complexity.

Fascinated by new technologies, Hanna realized the possibilities in equipment like the music program ProTools. With a highly debilitating diagnosis of Lyme's disease, through which she was supported by her husband Adam Horowitz of the Beastie Boys, it was a relief for Hanna to find new musical techniques that she could work with at home. In subsequent bands, starting with the intimate Julie Ruin with Johanna Fateman, which grew into the more dance-flavored Le Tigre and included Sadie Benning and J. D. Samson, she explored digital techniques and the new empowerment they were bringing to women musicians working from home. For Le Tigre, she cut tape with a razor and spliced it, old-school, before putting it into ProTools. Still hands-on, DIY—back to where it all began.

> You could make a drum beat out of found objects. Play guitar, and cut and paste it. It was much more like a fanzine

for me. I talked about Julie Ruin in terms of how fanzines sometimes would leave marks on, so people were reminded that human hands were behind the project; it's so important, it inspires women, gay kids—someone made this in their bedroom and I can make it in mine, without a studio or a major label record deal. It was incredibly scary to put out. I had no idea what the reaction would be. People hated it at first, but now it's regarded as marking a shift, when punks started to make electronic music. I just made it to stay sane.

* * *

Circumstances drove Kathleen Hanna to reprogram herself along with the technology. Her exploratory steps helped expand electronica and answer the question of how original, self-defined music might sound, if only women got to make it and people got to hear it. Discovering one's own sound, like a writer finding her voice, is an accumulation of such individual, intuitive steps over the edge, trusting in one's own velocity to find a flight path. Few artists enjoyed as many stylistic leaps as Manhattan's French import Lizzy Mercier Descloux. Paris has an unsung role in punk; the movement ultimately flopped because the national characteristic of "BCBG"—"bon chic, bon genre," understated, appropriate chic—could never make a safety pin seem anything other than artful. But Mercier Descloux and her then boyfriend, Michel Esteban, had helped kickstart the Paris scene with their punk style and sounds store Harry Cover—till the pair blithely shut it to split and taste downtown Manhattan's taboo honey in 1977.

Like so many, the Parisian pair were drawn by the freedom of the poly-arts whirlpool of New York's Lower East Side, where the subways never stopped and bodegas never closed, so unlike stuffy old Paris. Below Fourteenth Street, days bled into nights and dawns of wandering the streets of Soho and the Lower East Side, dipping and diving into bars, after-hours clubs, S&M and drag dives, and punk rock joints like CBGB, restlessly roaming among grimy tenements and dusty storefronts that artists could still seize as laboratories—where junkies thought they were geniuses and sometimes actually were. Mercier Descloux came to Manhattan to find her voice, and instead discovered that she contained many. Genre-flitting, she could commit herself only to engaging intensely with every moment, like her hero, the glamorous doomed poet Arthur Rimbaud, who set a rock-star template by living fast and dying young. Her then BFF Patti Smith shared that passion, and they recorded his poetry together. Smith illustrated Mercier Descloux's 1977 poetry chapbook, *Desiderata*. With matching shaggy, dark, androgynous hair, they laughed through photo-shoots, Smith in an askew confirmation frock, Mercier Descloux a roué in a man's tuxedo.

Shared creation can be erotic, yet more than most, Mercier Descloux's career was shaped by her man of the moment, be it Esteban (already an ex when they began recording) or British producer Adam Kidron, who made both 1984's *Zulu Rock* and their jazz experiment *One for the Soul* the next year (for which she managed to enlist legendary trumpeter Chet Baker). Kidron turned up the volume on Esteban's demands for her to sing—well, "better." Note the quotes. Like most punks, Mercier Descloux wasn't a conventionally "good" singer, but she knew how to make the most of her voice.

Another of her "collabolovers" was New York musician and artist Seth Tillett, who shot many of her first defining images. "Yes, she was a siren," he says. "Men crashed on those rocks." Call Mercier Descloux a dilettante, but hovering between possibilities in music, art, poetry, and film, the scrappy No Wave aesthetic suited her (she appears in underground director Amos Poe's *Blank Generation*). Yet men were often first drawn to her look. And looks. Tillett fell at first sight, at a concert by her then boyfriend, poet and musician Richard Hell. "Lizzy's eyes and eyebrows were incredible; she had this gigantic silver hair, skintight harlequin checkerboard pants. She was the most amazing thing I had ever seen," wondered Tillett. Richard Hell relished the stage clothes she made him and modeled his novel's love interest on her, but he emailed me, "I was never conscious of her musical career."

While Hell wasn't looking, Mercier Descloux hurled herself into punk. The thrill of her hunt (for herself?) resonates in her first music record, the Rosa Yemen EP by the two-guitar duo of herself and Michel's brother, Didier. The results are shards, cave drawings of directions, perfect in their wacky brevity, each a neon pointer to another way of making music. As an artifact, it suffers or benefits from multiple personalities, depending on your point of view. The duo's name evokes anarchists like Rosa Luxemburg and the divisive, violent native German terrorists/liberation fighters, the Baader-Meinhof Gang.

"Lizzy was incredibly intuitive and cool. I felt most strongly about Rosa Yemen. Those tracks were skankier, dirtier, sexier," recalls Ze Records label founder and head, Michael Zilkha. "They had a great sense of rhythm, space, and dynamic—untutored and completely wild. The tracks don't have a rhythmic base, which was the premise of Ze at the time."

Proudly primitive, Dada in its absurdity, their "Rosa Vertov" is a warped reflection of jazz innovator Ornette Coleman's harmolodic concept of the equality of sound. The track hits you like one of those drugs that speed-washes your mind; it blasts you to transcendence for seconds, then dumps you back in "reality," bewildered but elated. Like a shaman seized by strange passions, Mercier Descloux babbles incomprehensible incantations peppered with paranoid allusions to crime, journalists, cops . . . as if lit by a pulsing strobe, she dodges the rhythmic assault course for one and a half minutes. It is the going nuclear sound of an artist dropping the bomb on her musical identity.

On her quest for her musical self, Mercier Descloux successfully threaded her own poetic, anxious identity into her most commercially successful music, cut in different tropics: her 1981 Compass Point All-Stars collaboration "Mambo Nassau," made with the eclectic crew of session players assembled by Chris Blackwell that also delivered hits from Tom Tom Club and Grace Jones; and her South African recording, 1983's *Zulu Rock*, in which she arguably sounds happiest on what became her biggest hit, "Ou Sont Passées Les Gazelles," her faithful remake of a local Shanga'an disco hit by Obed N'gobengi and the Kurhula Sisters, "Ku Hluvukile Eka 'Zete.'"

"Lizzy was as alive in Soweto as she ever was in the downtown New York scene," says her friend Linnaea Tillett, the sister of Seth Tillet. "She was just on fire in that period—as though she had found home in a way. Lizzy was a complex, political, engaged sort of person. She wanted to use her music to draw attention to apartheid."

Ultimately, having released five albums of wildly varying styles connected mainly by their idiosyncrasy, the music business spat out the unorthodox artist in the late 1980s. She spent her last years painting and died in her beloved Corsica in 2004 at age 46. Girlfriends insist she was on the verge of a possible return to music, that young indie labels were seeking her as the missing link she was. Precisely because of its mood swings, one arty young French punkette's quest for her voice over six albums illustrates the question of the first punk girls' unprecedented generation: How will our music sound, with pretty much zero foremothers to draw from and respond to?

* * *

With her enthusiastic flexibility, who knows what sounds Lizzy Mercier Descloux might have made in the silent years? The roar of a creative personality defining itself, separating itself from its formation and becoming an individual, recognizable entity sounds like a vast iceberg ripping apart from its old glacier. Constant evolution marked Mercier Descloux's restless journey; for her, the easiest path seemed to be working with male Svengalis who seemed, then as now, to hold the key to the palace of paid art. She felt she needed them to mediate her career, and maybe she did. A decade after Mercier Descloux quit the industry—or vice versa—more open, less corporate spaces were opening up for female artists. Though slow, the progress of such countercultural channels proved beneficial for nonconforming girl players. They are often plunged into a fraught tango with the dominant patriarchy, a daily negotiation to lay claim to and broaden the boundaries of their autonomy. Separatism is a proven part of many a revolutionary struggle, and in the battle for creative self-determination, those gatekeeping boys can be gal-traps. While gathering that crucial trustworthy tribe, you have to be ready to go it alone. Both New York's Tamar-kali and London's Chardine Taylor-Stone of Big Joanie take their themes from aloneness and the particular stresses of a woman fending for herself, solo.

Compromise was never Tamar-kali's style, as one can hear in 2014's "Pearl." The track rolls out vigorous, forthright, guitar-driven power-punk springing from a propulsive chord change to tell the story of a girl making her way in the big, dangerous city alone. Its strength and tense energy convey Tamar-kali's own conflict-driven musical development.

What is freedom, what is love
always some string attached—
some fuckin' catch
can't deal in dealings with no integrity
where is honor what is sincerity
sometimes this city really gets me down can't
　　see my way through it all

Recalling her musical start in the 1990s, Tamar-kali says, "I didn't bring my sexuality to the agenda; I had a lot of boy envy. I had to make sure that I did not have a marginalized experience because of my gender. So I became super aggressive. I came into my own, and that's when problems arose. I broke up with my first hardcore band because of the gender thing." Her male band resented the only female player in the group talking gender and race politics from the stage. "But because of the uniqueness of the situation, I found a camaraderie with 'sistergirls' like singer Honeychile Coleman, Dunia Best from the ska-punk band Agent 99, and singer/bass player Felice Rosser of the band Faith."

Rich and robust, her brown velvet vocals bring an ancestral energy to her Brooklyn-born punk rock, established publicly in 1993. As her name suggests, Tamar-kali brings together global goddess energies, including not just her church training but the orishas of African spirituality and the Gullah community and language that are her maternal inheritance. Part of the Great Migration, her mother carried the Gullah spirit with her—along with a box of fried chicken!—on the long bus ride up from the South.

The Gullah community is one of America's best-known enclaves of African culture, preserved by enslaved Africans and their descendants along the coast of Georgia and the Carolinas. There, they had sufficient distance from the dominant culture to be able to preserve aspects of African language, food, and arts that were often beaten out of others in more populated areas. Among the Gullah, before the civil rights era, explains Tamar-kali, people wouldn't pay for the government bus that trundled across from the mainland. "They boycotted that thing way in advance," she says. "They put it out of business."

"In the punk rock scene, I gravitated to its aspects of Gullah culture that I saw when my mother sent me home for the summer. The isolation. Self-sufficiency. People working together. When I saw the DIY community working together, it made sense to me," she explains.

Operating as a male-mediated, multimedia outsider, reveling in her own exoticism, Lizzy Mercier Descloux chose to focus on music. But Tamar-kali's calling seems ordained. She was the adored childhood prodigy of an artistic family: her great-uncle is R&B hero Archie Bell of the Drells, her father is a jazz-funk drummer, and she taught herself guitar as a child. Still, Tamar-kali's journey to finding community was tortuous. "Catholic school taught me to resist," she says. One of the few nonwhites in the convent school classical choir, she got tucked away at the back, despite her undeniable voice. At home, she fell into a diasporic culture gap; most of her fellow Catholics were from the Caribbean, as were most of her Brooklyn neighbors, and they didn't get this Geechee warrior queen. First the pop-pier synthesizers of early 1980s new wave and then hardcore punk helped Tamar-kali see beyond the parochial confines that threatened to undermine her. "I developed a type of resistance and self-reliance," she says, "the determination that I AM going to make my way."

That passage was assisted by the explosion of America's Afropunk movement, a genuine people's outpouring that coalesced around the 2003 indie documentary by punk filmmaker James Spooner. A message board community sprang up around it, composed of African Americans and diasporic people who correctly felt institutionally excluded from the corridors of regular rock power. Their reach extended from the initial roots roster of local punk talent, including Tamar-kali, and broadened to give a new platform to Grace Jones, Lauryn Hill, Afro-futurist Janelle Monáe, neo-soul siren SZA, and actress/rapper Jean Grae. More corporate-minded forces saw the potential and Afropunk's brief was broadened and branded, finding an international festival community. With irony, Tamar-kali acknowledges that she was there "before it became a corporate shill!" Determinedly persisting, negotiating through each challenge to find a supportive scene and crew, Tamar-kali grew up to be a multimedia composer. But her bad punk self will not be subdued. "If you're punk rock, you're not looking for a leader anyway," she comments. "You make your own way."

* * *

A decade on and across the Atlantic Ocean, a parallel tussle with being lone outsiders also moved a quite different group of activist musicians in Brixton, South London. Despite her thematic connection to Tamar-kali, Chardine Taylor-Stone of Big Joanie forcefully states, "I don't want to be confused or conflated with African American narratives. There are similarities to our experience, but for us in the UK, the class divide can in some cases be bigger than the racial one. A family like mine, with a white grandmother, cousins, and aunties, is not unusual here."

Nonetheless, aloneness in a busy city is a great leveler. "The single woman has always been stigmatized as a lonely old spinster with too many cats," observes Kate Bolick in her book *Spinster: Making a Life of One's Own*. Sketching a state of dynamic change, Big Joanie's narcotic, undulating, feedback-drenched drone on 2016's "Dream Number 9" compels the listener to concentrate. The mournful but resolute voice intones, "All by myself. . . . despite myself, only dreaming, half here half full."

The song is steeped in isolation, which might or might not be lonely. Says drummer Taylor-Stone, "It is about being okay being on your own even if you are feeling a bit low. Too often women's happiness is tied into their relationships with men. I'm a lesbian, so I don't really have that issue as much; however, even with that, we are still expected to be in relationships. But the lyrics say, 'Despite myself I'm alright . . .'"

Big Joanie's funk is drenched through with industrial noise, in a direct line of descent from ESG, the pioneering Scroggins sisters of the Bronx, who brought their minimalist trio to downtown avant-garde rock clubs like Hurrah's and the Mudd Club in the 1980s. However, Taylor-Stone's experience is quite unlike those sisters', who were unique in their generation, or that of Tamar-kali, the Gullah woman warrior struggling to find her crew. Growing up in twenty-first-century Britain, the various tribes impacting her life were friendly, and Taylor-Stone has the support of a network of feminist artists.

As one of the newest, youngest bands in this book, Big Joanie arguably benefits from the fighting spirit of their musical fore-mothers like Tamar-kali. Engaged as artist, intellectual, and activist, Taylor-Stone has a clarity about her mixed identity that is far from the turmoil that, say, Poly Styrene went through.

"As a band, I guess our existence challenges certain tropes. The assumption that we must be influenced by reggae is interesting to me, and it doesn't allow much space for us to be influenced by other things, which we are," states Taylor-Stone.

All our band grew up in punk, and I was also in the rocka-billy scene. Within our own community we are sometimes forced to be restricted in our tastes, as anything outside of hip-hop, reggae, grime, or R&B is deemed "white." With Big Joanie, we challenge that! How can you say we make "white music," when we are so obviously black and our politics are black centered? We are far more radical than some hip-hop artists who aspire to "succeed" within a white supremacist gaze, consciously making their music palatable for middle-of-the-road white audiences. We don't make those allowances for anyone.

Taylor-Stone inhabits an arguably rarified, politically aware independent sector of the music industry. As an academic and researcher, she "collects oral histories of black British women who are/have been in subcultures and what that says about black British identity. With Big Joanie, we wanted to be a voice for people of color in a predominantly white scene, especially for women," she says. "I also do a lot of activism around black LGBTQ issues, which led to me winning a British LGBT award. Slightly bizarre. I can feel myself being absorbed into the establishment, but sometimes you have got to make change from the inside."

* * *

Working at a time when the agenda that compels Chardine Taylor-Stone—identity issues of race, gender and class—has become so hotly debated, she is able to build on an existing framework and establish her own place within it. Such access both in and out of the establishment was rarely if ever permitted to previous generations of female punks. "A woman must have money and a room of her own if she is to write fiction," Virginia Woolf wrote in 1929. The same applies to being a musician, in that Woolf really means autonomy, making your own space in which to create, however you succeed in contriving it. The familiar Riot Grrrl cry "Girls to the front!" was designed to stop a leaping, frenzied, all-male mosh pit from preventing women from enjoying the show without getting smashed by a random pumping fist: a common complaint from girl punk fans.

Over and over, She-Punks shout for their own space, which translates as agency. No wonder, then, that groups like the Delta 5 in 1970s Leeds and the Bush Tetras in early 1980s downtown New York both sang about getting people out of their face.

"Everyone called us a woman's band, which is kind of a misinterpretation, because we always had two guys in the group," sighs Bethan Peters, the Australia-born, New Zealand-raised bass player of the Delta 5 who really grew up as a law student/punk musician in Leeds. "Mind Your Own Business" was released in 1979, a pivotal moment in England. The knock-on effect of repeated strikes led to what was called the Winter of Discontent, with its collapse of basic social services and approximation of anarchy, leading to the election of Conservative leader Margaret Thatcher. It was the abandonment of an idea of egalitarian socialism that had failed to align itself with the future of industry and business, particularly new technology. Its replacement was a hysterically optimistic conservatism. In a domino effect, Thatcherite promises of a more dynamic capitalism with home ownership for all led to the economic devastation of the old working-class industrial North of England. As its music reflects, Leeds was in the forefront of anti-establishment thinking, with a vigorous breed of no-nonsense student Lefties. Women's rights were a default belief for them, in contrast to the chauvinism usually ascribed to old-school Northern blokes. Alongside singer Julz Sale, the band included drummer Kelvin Knight and guitarist Alan Riggs. The women of the Delta 5 blossomed alongside their supportive male mates, unlike so many women artists here. Their spiky, metallic, grating guitar sound expresses the feel of that group of artists: rigorous, uncompromising, their arrogant conceptualism tempered with welcome sarcasm.

"We all met in Leeds; the Mekons, the Gang of Four, and us were all still students at college in Leeds. I finished my degree in 1978 and stayed on after; our other bass player, Ros Allen, was doing a fine arts degree," Peters reminisces from her village home in *la France profonde*, where she works from home as a high-level technology legal consultant. "It was all very interconnected. We were all going out with each other, mixed up like a big huge group of friends. The Gang of Four signed to EMI quite early. They had money, which was unheard of. We used their facilities and did our own thing, then we went out on our own and did gigs by ourselves, rushing up and down the motorway in a van."

The genesis of "Mind Your Own Business" was communal, as befit the times. The music and arrangement was by the Delta 5, but those tough girl lyrics were written by a boy whom they never actually met.

Someone showed us these lyrics written by Simon Best, a guy from the Leeds scene. I don't think we analyzed it too much; it was grab it and use it. If it had been obnoxious, we wouldn't have touched it, but it was really quite good. It did apply to the boy/girl thing, but it could also be about anyone, which was quite nice. Immediately we put together the bass line and split it into two between Roz's fretless bass and my treble. In fact, the very first time we played it was with Dave Allen, the bass player from the Gang of Four, so it probably has some of their energy.

The peremptory oddness of the space-asserting, angry lyrics, more barked than sung by the two girls, the rounded yet still industrial edge to the neo-funk bass, the crisp detachment and repeated silvery shiver of the drums' hi-hat cymbal, followed by a drastic, dub-by instrumental dropout which leaves the drummer working feet instead of hands in a martial command—and of course, those jangling, minor key guitars vying with each other in an itchy rhythm . . . with all its snotty attitude, the success of "Mind Your Own Business" comes also from how the instruments match the words' imperious demands. These were truly Rude Girls.

Can I have a taste of your ice cream?
Can I lick the crumbs from your table?
Can I interfere in your crisis?

No, mind your own business

"How it came out was lack of technique more than anything," Peters admits. "We had a rudimentary approach to everything, and we blurted it out quite baldly. Us whooping was quite fun; we improvised at the time and it stuck. That was how we did things."

Let's hear it for female-friendly fellers and the relative prevalence of, or at least attempts at, gender equality among the more socialist-leaning enclaves. Given the avalanche of mostly man-made sorrow that Kathleen Hanna had to try and fix with Riot Grrrl, a herculean task, it's something of a relief to be reminded of how easily the genders can get along.

"We always had loads of fanboys who would follow us 'round to all our gigs, and nobody tried anything; we had serious attitude and they were all too much in awe," Peters says. "It was hilarious. Guys would come back and say hello in America, and give us things. We had completely no issues with us getting hassled at all. Except for the one gig that we did in Palo Alto, where some mini-fascists were making trouble at the front and I stopped playing and told them to eff off. Guys give us grief? God no, they wouldn't dare!"

*   *   *

Independent and feisty to the bone: that was the default position of UK She-Punks, in parallel to the scrappy attitude of the boys. However, apart from the threat of random IRA bombings, street riots around the country, the regular fights between various youth tribes and the police, and confrontations at demonstrations, life was comparatively peaceful—or at least it wasn't like a rerun of a vampire movie, as scenes in the Lower East Side sometimes appeared to be.

The Lower East Side, where so much of New York's punk rock found a home, was low rent. To sleep in summertime, families would crowd mattresses onto the fire escapes that zigzagged up the nineteenth-century redbrick tenements. Little electric fans from the 99-cent store couldn't defeat the stifling heat, even after dark. Lower East Side nights back then, pre-gentrification, were less innocent than those of UK punks. While Brits might run the gauntlet of racists or other hostile youth gangs, or the police, getting home after a gig for most young punks meant staggering onto the top deck of the last late-night bus, maybe scoring a snog on the back seat. But after, say, 1:00 a.m., many of the under-lit blocks in the Lower East Side, some of which were squats, actually were scary—unless you were looking to score heroin, and even then. Burned-out buildings often suspected to be landlord insurance scams had left the area almost as scarred as London after the Blitz bombings. And the downtown pleasure dome often sheltered too many real downers, figurative and literal. A good number of punk artists flirted with and were made mad or dead by heroin. Arguably, its use was falsely glamorized by its association with local artistic heroes such as writer William Burroughs and jazz musician John Coltrane. However, together with the scare factor of jonesing junkies and vicious dealers was the way that New York was also more art conscious than other punk centers, including London. The presence of Andy Warhol's Factory and its works canteen, Max's Kansas City club near Union Square, was still perceived as setting a creative gold standard, even after the artist's death.

Like so many of their peers, the Bush Tetras were drawn to New York's art scene from elsewhere. Friends Cynthia Sley and Laura Kennedy both dropped out of art school in Cleveland. "I came to New York to have a career in art," says Sley. "I landed in the East Village and Soho when there was a lot of really cool music." Explains guitarist Pat Place, "I came to New York from Chicago in 1975 because I was interested in performance and conceptual art. Basically, I crossed over from art when I met James Chance and joined the Contortions." After the end of that twisted neo-jazz ensemble, the friends and jamming partners were soon reconfigured as the Bush Tetras.

"Those were the days!" Place laughs. "It couldn't happen now. When we started in 1979, things were very different. Living on the Lower East Side, you could have a little job and play music the rest of the time."

The first verse of the song that came to define them, 1981's "Too Many Creeps," was written by Place in the ticket booth at the Bleecker Street Theatre, where she and Kennedy worked. "We were freaks, and we would get hassled if we left the East Village—and even there," she laments. To some, the girls cut an intimidating figure. "We were pretty sassy and people were scared of us. We were attacked and had a hard time," Sley says. "With our short haircuts, people could not figure out if we were boys or girls."

I just don't wanna go
Out in the streets no more
Because these people they give me
They give me the creep . . . s

I don't wanna
Too many creeps

Snotty, bratty, and undeniably cool, the vocals dripping disdain over a ripped-and-torn rhythm, the track had an irresistible bad girls' attitude. They scored a deal with indie label 99 Records, run by Ed Bahlman and his partner Gina Franklyn out of a basement record-cum-clothing store at 99 Bleecker Street. Thus the Bush Tetras became part of a community that included bands like Bronx future funk queens ESG, mass guitar symphonist Glenn Branca (and this writer).

Their rise was precipitate. In February 1980, Kennedy, Place, Sley, and Dee Pop opened up for 8 Eye Spy at the cozy Tier 3—then just days later, they were opening for far better-known groups the Feelies and DNA at a significantly larger venue, Irving Plaza. Sley was so shocked she forgot to turn up her guitar, but Place played extra forcefully and no one noticed.

The Bush Tetras were acclaimed as among the most progressive of the New York post-punk bands. Theirs was a small world whose music rang loudly in the ears of eager international music fans; their domain consisted of the blocks below Manhattan's Fourteenth Street, above which was considered "nosebleed territory" by scenesters. Experimental, edgy, and confrontational, spiked with their local New York funk, the Bush Tetras fit perfectly with British bands like the Delta 5 and the Gang of Four. After punk's primal thrash, post-punks were keen to explore more rhythmic complexities. Yet they knew the implications of their singularity.

Says Pat Place, "It was a little different in our scene because there were more girls in bands." The scene had created space for distinctive artists like Ann Magnusson's collective/band, Pulsallama, Ut, Adele Bertei, and Lydia Lunch. Still, Place says, "I would definitely get attitude from male guitarists and soundmen about women playing guitar—as in, they can't."

Given the very exhausting circumstances of life in the post-punk fast lane, perhaps the outcome was inevitable. "We'd been on the road for three years and we were all burned out," says Place. "There were some drugs involved. That was what was going on. Drugs were flowing, part of the whole deal. I just collapsed in the end." Like the frenzied, fabulous scene from which they came, soon to be decimated by AIDS and Giuliani's imperious mayoral anti-nightlife agenda, the Bush Tetras had largely succeeded in asserting their particular louche tough girl, downtown cool persona. Within the hip confines of the Lower East Side, whose hedonistic mores helped lead to the band's demise in 1983, they imploded under the strains of underground stardom. Yet, as noted often here, with the revival of interest in original She-Punks, the Bush Tetras began to play again and released an EP, "Take the Fall," that broke a decade's silence—they had carved a legitimate space for their cutting, deadpan hip.

* * *

The imperative for female space is nowhere more evident than the dance floor. For girls, being hit or kicked by pogoing blokes in a club, accidentally or not, or worse, groped by drunken strangers, is a (literally) painful intrusion that, worse, denotes contempt and the near-invisibility of women to the perpetrators. Worse, it is a metaphor for the inequities of society, when even in the "rich" world, women routinely earn less than men, see few like them in powerful positions, and, after all these centuries, still have to struggle to be able to do what they want with their own bodies.

Make room for Fea from San Antonio, Texas. A common nightlife harassment scenario is vivid in their 2016 "Mujer Moderna" ("Modern Woman") video, wherein the forceful band let their harassers know who's boss. Crude abusers have to step back. Defining their modernity and giving Fea support in the club is the unusual sight of a neon Virgin of Guadalupe. "I don't believe my mother thought we would make music a career. I'm sure she thought I would marry and have a baby. It was the structure in our family," says drummer Phanie Diaz.

> You can't control it and you want it for free
> I'm not a slut, I'm not a hooker,
> I am a modern woman

Power-driven by Diaz and bass player Aaron Magaña, Fea almost verge on pop; harmonic guitar and vocal lines on "Mujer Moderna" mark them out as unusually tuneful for such heavy rockers. No wonder, as Diaz, whose drummer father is one among several musicians in the family, grew up hearing them play emotional Tejano and conjunto tunes at home—though she has never played with them. Most punkily, Fea means "ugly," challenging pop star norms à la Poly Styrene. Fea were aware of their "ancestors," they say, such as the Riot Grrrls and even the original UK punkettes like the Raincoats and the Slits.

However, as Chicana (female descendants of Mexican immigrants) musicians, a solitary Hispanic star twinkled in the young artists' firmament—Alicia Velasquez, a.k.a. Alice Bag of the first-wave Los Angeles mid-1970s punk scene favorites the Bags. "She loved punk. She wanted to play. She gave it just as hard as the men and still does," exclaims Diaz. "To see a woman of color on stage is even more of a push to marginalized people that anyone can do it. Your race, look, size doesn't matter. Just do it," she urges. "We have to acknowledge that as women in music, in general, we are treated as lesser than. It's assumed that men know more about their instruments and will play it better. We are also supposed to have a 'look.' Like women in music are a gimmick. This is not the case, and the more we bring it to light in song and in person, the more others will realize that women are not a gimmick. Maybe we can teach you something."

Jenn Alva and Phanie Diaz have been jamming since they sat next to each other at middle school; Diaz was already into punk and played guitar. Swift accomplices, they formed bands.

"We pretty much taught ourselves on stage. It was always by ear." After the folky feel of Girl in a Coma, built around the vocals of Phanie's sister Nina, the sisters tapped into their tougher side with Fea—and have kept Girl in a Coma alive too.

"Texas is definitely a macho state," says Diaz. "The women were always cooking. Growing up there as Latinas, it was ordinary for them to serve the men first, before sitting down to eat themselves. But I grew up with a vision of music and knew no barriers, even if it was a male-dominated career."

Happily for Fea, like their contemporaries Big Joanie in London they benefitted from an established sisterhood of older musicians, particularly the ones who had inspired them. Their mother introduced them to the Runaways' Joan Jett, who signed Girl in a Coma, then Fea, to her own Blackheart label and enlisted Alice Bag to co-produce their album. They reaped the rewards of hard-won battles. They have found a way to function somewhat independently and developed their own audience and market, so their survival is not dependent on success in the mainstream majority commercial arena. "Being a queer, Latina, thick woman, I felt the world was against us. We were judged as too fat or too gay," Diaz concludes. "Whatever it was, it didn't and doesn't faze us. We just know we love to play and we will; and if another girl sees us up there and we are just like them, that's the mission. Eventually everyone will see a musician and not just a woman up there. A strong musician."

* * *

Since the mid-1970s and the dawn of female punk, women have been fluidly using the full-frontal genre to outwit their ever-evolving, many-fronted challenges. Invariably, they have to battle to make music their way—and sometimes also struggle to find out what that way is. There has been some successful selling of the rebel girl archetype: a mass audience for some contrarian punkettes, a motley crew operating within various styles. United in bucking the norm, their faces still fit. Excellence helps. They include artists as different and distinctive as Luscious Jackson (who helped segue punk into hip-hop), Deborah Ann Dyer a.k.a. Skin, Pink, Icona Pop, M.I.A., Beth Ditto, Bjork, the Noisettes' Shingai Shoniwa, Kelis, Kesha, Meshell Ndegeocello, FKA Twigs, Janelle Monáe, Santigold, Angel Haze, and Princess Nokia. Nonetheless, as the heart of punk is always with the marginals, let us also consider the weird ones who don't fit the still often male/reductive multinational concept of what girl act will work this season. Arguably that is the female punk majority: seen as less palatable to the mainstream despite quality and originality, so never even tested.

We must make a place in a market manipulated to pander to the clichéd male gaze; find a voice for our feelings when we've never heard anyone sound the way we hear in our head; break generations of our family's female mode of being; construct new forms of family and effective motherhood; position ourselves within the newly possible flexing of gender experimentation and fight for the right to do so. All this while adapting to changing projections of girly sexuality, from 1950s repression to the free love, polyamorous flirtations of the 1960s, '70s, and early '80s—flirtations that would mutate into the twenty-first century's acrobatic, pornographic smorgasbord of internet lust. This very different sort of pressure on teenage girls led to a mid-twenty-first-century rise in the sort of self-harm that in a 1976 club bathroom shocked Poly Styrene into defying the bondage of society's norms. With all of that, particularly in politically progressive and, yes, often leftist circles, outside of the mainstream conveyor belt industry, supposedly marginal twenty-first-century girls committed to their music can find a support system and a platform their predecessors could only dream of. Hope is not a joke.

LINEUP & TRACK LISTING:

1. Patti Smith, "Free Money" (US, 1975)
The shamanistic poet and punk avatar digs deep for a poignant paean to the illusory dreams of what money can bring.

2. Malaria!, "Geld" ("Money") (Germany, 1983)
From the radical artistic ferment of Berlin in the last years of the wall, Malaria! despise how the other less-than-half live.

3. ESG, "Earn It" (US, 1981–1992)
The Scroggins sisters from the Bronx projects bring the barrio into downtown post-punk funk, energizing hip-hop.

4. Shonen Knife, "New Find" (Japan, 1992)
Two Osaka sisters' cheery pop-punk tribute to life's simple, inexpensive pleasures.

5. The Slits, "Spend, Spend, Spend" (UK, 1979)
Redolent of Weimar cabaret, these prototypical She-Punks question their urge to consume and their hunger, physical and metaphorical.

6. Pussy Riot, "Kropotkin Vodka" (Russia, 2012)
The once-anonymous agit-punk female collective invokes a mythical liquor that will inflame the masses to overthrow the oligarchs.

7. Maid of Ace, "Made in England" (UK, 2016)
Sisters from Hastings, a vacation town fallen on hard times, celebrate the joys of their underclass ducking and diving post-jobs economy lifestyle.

2

MONEY

Are We Our Stuff?

There is a clear continuum from the feminization of poverty to the masculinization of wealth. It's no accident.

Gloria Steinem, *Moving Beyond Words*, 2012

"HERE, TRY IT ON!" the punk poetess Patti Smith urged me. Together with the photographer Dennis Morris and her guitarist Lenny Kaye, we were sifting the racks of a Japanese store, unusual for the times, in West London's Notting Hill Gate. It was 1976, and Smith had recently begun to find herself in an unusual position for a native of the counterculture—making unprecedented cash from her first LP, *Horses*, a surprise critical and commercial success. Being a leftist bohemian, she was showing generous integrity by doing something unexpected—she bought both myself and Morris a proper present.

Smith wanted to spread her largesse, and being a writer herself for *Creem* magazine as well as a published poet, she did not regard the rock media as dodgy lackeys to be ducked, but rather cultural workers like herself. Her gracious gift, a zip-front, black velvet quilted Mao jacket piped in red, was actually a bit boxy— but I wore it for years. After all, Patti Smith got it for me. And besides—it was free!

Smith would be garlanded with awards including the French Ordre des Arts et des Lettres in 2005, the National Book Award for her 2010 memoir *Just Kids*, and membership in the Rock and Roll Hall of Fame. She continues to help artists, now on a somewhat larger scale; in 2017 she bought the reconstructed chateau of her great inspiration, the poet Rimbaud, on the Franco-Belgian border. It was there that Rimbaud wrote his "Seasons of Hell" at just nineteen years old, the match that lit a brief but incandescent life. His intensity, the idea of living life ablaze even if you are extinguished too soon, has always inspired Smith. As we wandered back down Portobello Road to her hotel from Notting Hill with our shopping bags, she told me, "I don't have a stage persona or a record persona, not one that's separate from myself."

When we chatted on that sunlit afternoon, a British woman's right to sign for her own bank loan without consent from a father or husband had only been legal a year; a further four would pass before risqué boundary-flexer Madonna would wittily bitch-slap the old association of punk females and the anti-consumerist counterculture with "Material Girl"; ironic or not, her compelling persona helped to hustle in a new, Reagan/Thatcherite, more me-centric groove. Unlike the Raincoats, more like her fellow New Yorkers Blondie, in the song's video, Madonna exuberantly channels tropes of 1950s sexuality—notably our sacrificial blonde Marilyn Monroe, both brazen and demure as she purrs, "Diamonds Are a Girl's Best Friend" in 1953. Of her complex array of personae, that specific Madonna moment signaled, winking: Who cares that Congress just rejected the Equal Rights Amendment! We still have our old-school feminine wiles! Onscreen, our Ma-Mas, Madonna and Marilyn, flaunted parrot-bright satin, red and hot pink. By contrast, as we traipsed into the Portobello Hotel lobby, Patti Smith was wearing an oversize man's dark jacket that could have been borrowed off a scarecrow. The radical newness of her downbeat, un-girly-girl image would remain her "look" and be a consistent aesthetic foil for Madonna's decades of frisky ego games.

That monochrome, boyish severity signals Smith's integrity and authenticity, to both her and her audience. Reliably, every show is a commitment and a communion, in which she appears to strip her spirit down to below the bone, reaching for shamanistic revelation and rebirth. After she fell off the stage in a show in Florida in 1977 and broke several vertebrae, narrowly avoiding death or paralysis, she spoke to me at the *Sounds* office in then-shabby Covent Garden, long distance on the transatlantic telephone. "I was spinning like a dervish—you've seen me do that. I'm like the kind of performer that courts risk, I court death," she proclaimed. The Field Marshal, as she called herself, saw the legendary white light—but was called back to round up her troops once more.

For the writer and performer of "Free Money," the ability to be free with money (as opposed to money being free) was an expansive rejection of the frugality she had grown up with in her hardscrabble New Jersey working-class family. The sight of her mother painstakingly sticking the stamps for "free" giveaways, trying to stretch the family's meagre resources as best she could in a system designed to never let her get ahead, infuses "Free Money" with a piercing elegiac yearning.

> Every night before I rest my head
> See those dollar bills go swirling 'round my bed
> I know they're stolen, but I don't feel bad
> I take that money, buy you things you never had
> Oh, baby, it would mean so much to me
> Oh, baby, to buy you all the things you need for free

Starting with fragility, over piano player Richard "DNV" Sohl's lyrical triplets, Smith's gentle vibrato caresses the lines, drawing the listener in until, quite smoothly, the speed builds, just like the whirling dervish she said she channels on stage; rock 'n' roll propulsion kicks in, with its smart changes and statement drum fills by Jay Dee Daugherty. Then it is right into overdrive, pushed by Lenny Kaye's urgently scratched chords and, having described the material delights she wishes she could offer, Smith chants the title repeatedly, the Field Marshal calling on all to find the spirit within themselves which is their true engine, and the real moneymaker to shake. It has remained in her set for four decades, and she renews its meaning each time it is performed. For Patti Smith, all the pain that rises in the chest and blocks the throat when one longs to save a beloved and money would make all the difference is palpable in every performance of "Free Money."

The career of 1980s New York artist Carl Apfelschnitt (lost to AIDS too young) was buoyed by rich patrons, and he would comment, "Money is love in action." So it can even be for an anarchist, as when Vi Subversa came into an inheritance and was able to fund Crass' first 45. Smith's early "outsider" period was well spent preparing for a lifetime of making a variety of art.

Like all conscious first-generation punks shaped by the student riots of the 1960s in London and Paris, Smith was touched by the free-living, free-loving ideas of the Situationists, like Guy Debord, and their illustrated cartoon-style injunctions made to startle, like "Beneath the paving stones—the beach!" Her approach to life and art was bold, exploratory, fulfilling the movement's agit-art manifesto from May 1960: "At a higher stage, everyone will become an artist, i.e. inseparably a producer-consumer of total culture creation, which will help the rapid dissolution of the linear criteria of novelty. Everyone will be a situationist, so to speak, with a multi-dimensional inflation of tendencies, experiences, or radically different 'schools'—not successively, but simultaneously."

Thanks to talent and timing, Smith transcended the general fate of mid-1970s women. It was only when the decade hustled its way into the next "me-terial" decade that gender income equality started to move more briskly. Between 1978 and 1990, the game of catch-up took us from a tragic 61 percent pay gap to a still utterly weedy and inexcusable 76.5 percent of what men got. And after that, things flatlined. Female incomes froze while males' rose—just in time for the 1990s Riot Grrrls to feel it. Add to that, these women are artists and determined to remain so, which is a job in itself, though one whose financial rewards have historically been unpredictable, whatever your gifts. As fear battles with surveillance and danger to see which will drive the civil liberties of our international capitals, and scuzzy bohemia from Paris's Les Halles and New York's Lower East Side to London's Ladbroke Grove mutates into glossy condos—how much space will be left for budding artists to "duck and dive"? Nonconformity has been branded as a lifestyle just when it has largely been expelled from the big cities. However, committed female artists will find a way through, as Patti Smith did in her looser time. The story of female punks and money, as told in their music, is a template for our direction as a whole in this increasingly economically divided society.

Though closely associated with punk, Smith's creative credentials extend further back into the days of Andy Warhol, and before that to the beatnik bohemians she associated with: free spirits such as jazz icon Ornette Coleman, writer William Burroughs and poet Allen Ginsberg. Prior to becoming a rock star, she was a dramatist and working poet. By the time *Horses* rode in, Smith's countercultural standing reputation had translated to the growing first-wave New York punk scene. Its locus had also shifted, a few blocks down and east: from Warhol's silver-painted Factory off Union Square and its café, Max's Kansas City, down to the scuzzier, more easterly Bowery, then home to bums and drunks, and a grotty dive bar called CBGB, the mecca of downtown punk. She was joined there by the rest of the city's new wave—an artier marketing term for punk devised by Seymour Stein, the managing director of WEA/Sire Records, the label which signed a swathe of downtown New York cool-makers including Madonna and Talking Heads with their intense female bass player, Tina Frantz. Re-calling the marketing brainwave, Stein writes, "Nothing at all wrong with punk, but bands like Talking Heads, and there were others, were something different."

Vive la différence. A new breed of autonomous, self-defined, and uninhibited female rock star, in her creative partnership with

Robert Mapplethorpe, Smith did not shrink from exposing armpit hair or posing nude, more changeling than centerfold, oddly angled by a radiator on a wooden floor. Her portrait on *Horses*, in which she wears a man's open-neck white shirt and tie, slinging a jacket over her shoulder like an urchin Frank Sinatra, is watchful, knowing yet curiously innocent. The images made her as much of an androgynous icon as Jamaican multitalented artist Grace Jones, glowering in her low-cut tuxedo and flat-top hair, cigarette dangling dangerously, shot by Jean-Paul Goude.

Smith courted the edge. She had not specifically focused on making work calculated to attract money. No doubt she made artistic choices that she trusted would not alienate an audience, but she basically made the sound and told the stories she wanted to hear. As she chronicles in her memoirs, like any aspiring artist without family money, Smith knew how to enjoy life without necessarily having much financially. Playing it her way was of more significance, and appropriate material reward would hopefully follow.

* * *

The very year that Madonna's "Material Girl" helped move a generation into the malls, Berlin's experimental electronica post-punk band Malaria!, in 1983's "Geld" ("Money") claimed a leftist, ascetic anti-consumerism that Patti Smith and others would recognize. Foremothers of the German electronica scene, Malaria! were loosely associated with the German new wave, *Neue Deutsche Welle*, along with Ari Up's good friend, the colorful opera-trained extrovert Nina Hagen. Berlin has always been a magnet for louche bohemia, with its whiff of Weimar decadence, Brechtian experimentation, Cold War drama—and large, grand apartments at a cheap rent. (David Bowie had recently recorded his timeless trilogy there.) Escapees were still being shot dead trying to get to the West over the heavily guarded wall when

Malaria!'s founders, Bettina Köster and Gudrun Gut, fellow students at Berlin's Art University, made a video for "Money" with experimental Super 8 filmmaker friends Dieter Hormer and Brigitte Bühler. Extravagantly anti-naturalistic, it is an unabashed homage to the menace cast by the German expressionist films they loved, like Robert Wiene's 1920 *The Cabinet of Dr. Caligari*. Exaggerated stylization enabled auteurs to convey coded signals that the censor might have stopped in those immediate pre-Nazi years, and the guerilla subterfuge still resonated.

"In the frigid, prematurely middle aged cultural climate that was West Germany, the West Berlin underground prided itself on what an Einstürzende Neubauten song title later summarized as 'To Be No Part of It,' and Malaria! were very much in that spirit," says the editor of *The Wire* magazine, Chris Bohn, who chronicled the Berlin movement. "The women of Malaria! were of a generation resistant to the '60s and '70s virtuous right-on-ness of all things countercultural back then. Punk was a fantastic relief valve for them, and peer groups like Die Tödliche Doris and Einstürzende Neubauten, where Gudrun started."

"The scene Malaria! were part of was a fabulously exhilarating, bordering nihilistic, bourgeois-morality-free zone in the bizarro, walled-in island oasis of consumerism that was 1980s West Berlin, some one hundred miles deep inside the communist Deutsche Demokratische Republik. In that anarchist counter-culture, there was a whole lotta squatting going on," Bohn remembers.

Malaria! embraced being outsiders. "None of us had any money!" laughs Gudrun Gut. "There were no grants back then." Adds Bettina Köster, "We were all poor. Everybody with a job had left Berlin; the city had the highest alcohol consumption of the country. The boys from [local band] D.A.F. used to come by to pick up bottles to sell. But it was a special time. Everything was commerce free. It was all so free. It was good for the artistic aspect, as there was no commercial aspect. Painters did not have galleries, musicians did not have places to play, filmmakers wanted to show their movies; so we would band together and find a place where we could do it all, interdisciplinary." Community worked for Malaria!. Their original indie label album was made with the help of established local band Tangerine Dream, who offered their studio, and the women next worked with an independent Brussels label of note, Les Disques du Crépuscule. Eventually, Malaria! were able to control their catalog by purchasing their masters. In 1997 Gut launched her own label, Monika Enterprises, and managed Crépuscule's Moabit Musik; in 2017, Köster released an album, *Kolonel Silvertop*, and went on the road again.

Anticipating techno by years, the minimalism of Malaria! toys with sonic dimensions. They stab elastic synthesizer phrases that wobble like amoebae. Brutally battered one-rhythm drums support Köster's neurotic but proud vocals:

Attention! Attention!
Money rules the world
New religion, old religion
Our beliefs are our world
Our world is our money
I let myself be charmed. . . .

"The song questions the belief in money and the power of insurance companies whose executives live in mansions, and [is] about being lost in the fog [of materialism] and getting seduced," Gut explains. "And it is about how happy we would be if we were not so hungry."

The Malaria! song "Kaltes Klares Wasser" ("Cold Clear Water") was later covered by Alex Murray-Leslie and Melissa Logan of Chicks on Speed, the Berlin-based art-electro-punk feminist collective. Spearheaded by Murray-Leslie, their 2006 *Girl Monster* compilation was arguably the first to codify a coherent narrative of women in electronica and post-punk. The anthology was an activist response to the systemic methods of cultural control of women's work via erasure, which *The Beauty Myth* author Naomi Wolf describes thus: "The links between generations must always be newly broken."

In her own way, Gut countered this process by helping younger female artists like Chicks on Speed, as Tangerine Dream had helped them at the start. Murray-Leslie explains, "She was a major catalyst for us to start making music. Gudrun really encouraged us before we even had a group. She'd come to Ultraschall, a club where I was working at the time on the door, we'd all get into long conversations early into the morning and she'd give us 'assignments,' like get us to make mix tapes, that she'd then play on her radio station."

Reinterpreting Malaria!, Logan recalls, "was very difficult, because the feeling of the song was already so dominant: the dark and oh-so-cool lyrics, this sense of being aroused and slightly *kaput* [shattered] simultaneously. I think this feeling speaks for the girl punk/post-punk time; ecstatic but tough, oh-so-cool but cutting."

* * *

To be cool was to be real, a survival technique in an often hostile context, as the Bush Tetras observed of life in nosebleed country, above the gilded grid of New York's quasi-equal 1980s downtown. There in Punkzone, even if it wasn't fully manifest, at least gender equality was culturally understood as a shared theoretical goal. But way above even midtown's nosebleed country, in crack-ravaged Harlem and the neighboring Bronx, home of ESG (Emerald, Sapphire, and Gold), the Scroggins sisters' minimalist punk-funk band, the hostility was on a different level; the threat was more general and immediately physical, particularly for the youth.

Rejected for aid by the federal government, New York City was a national no-go zone, and its own Forbidden Cities were uptown: Harlem and particularly the Bronx. The Scroggins family was caught up in the regular infernos captured in the 1972 BBC documentary *The Bronx Is Burning*. In it, Upper Manhattan looks like Dresden after the Blitz—mostly just gone, looming skeletal remnants of buildings blasted into abstract sculpture. Often set for insurance, uptown's wanton arson and carnage occurred amid manipulated violence from gangs and drugs—coke, crack, angel dust. Some elder Scroggins siblings got hooked but ultimately escaped dope's shackles. Still, as if to bear out the scary adage about art blooming in adversity, the Bronx was creatively fertile, with graffiti brightening burned-out tenements, and always buoyed by glittering local Latin sounds like salsa and merengue. DJ Afrika Bambaataa was forming his Zulu Nation, spreading ideas of positive tribalism in the dawn of hip-hop. Amid the devastation, rebirth. It was a propitious moment for ESG, as messengers of a new polyglot aesthetic, to build their sonic bridge—nonetheless, a properly dangerous one.

The original band was all Scroggins siblings: singer Renée, drummer Valerie, bassist Deborah, and Marie on congas and backing vocals. Seeing them groove to music on TV, their mother, a clerk in the health department, took the bold step of buying them instruments to keep them off the streets. "It's always been harder for women to get out there. Back then, the only female-type act we knew was Labelle with Patti Labelle, a very powerful singer. And they broke up," Renée Scroggins points out.

Along with the Bush Tetras, who both inspired ESG and loaned them amps, they became part of downtown New York's post-punk/new wave circuit, playing fabled Manhattan venues like the Mudd Club and Hurrah in the early 1980s, then taking their tensile, pared-down punk-funk to Europe. As literal sisters, black girls, ESG were unique in their generation, the insufficiently sung foremothers of other groove-bending post-funk punks like London's Big Joanie and Skinny Girl Diet in the mid-2010s.

Effectively, ESG were executing the same process with live instruments that local DJs like Kool Herc and Bambaataa were developing in the new science of turntable skills: extending the rhythm breakdown section that usually demarcates a song's hook and chorus till it becomes the whole sound. The side dish becomes the main course.

The sisters were shy but clearly determined when I first met them in the basement offices of their (and my) label, 99 Records at 99 Bleecker Street; label boss Ed Bahlman was their manager. The narrow tenement space sold imports and punk on one side, with a treasure trove of vintage and locally made clothes sold by Gina Franklyn on the other. The ambiance was cozy, maybe because it was quite dark. A similar subterranean intimacy inhabits the blare of feedback, the slow burn of 1981's stripped-down, pungent "Moody," its light-fingered middle-eight conga breaks stinging, bringing the Latin barrio that ESG heard from their project windows into post-punk. A blast from the past and future, it became an underground classic, frequently recycled, and a house music staple. Later, they were picked up by Manchester's progressive dance/industrial label Factory Records before working with different indies and building their own networks. They may have smoldered, but ESG were never extinguished; in 2018 the band undertook an international tour that was sold out a year in advance.

"There are avenues today we never had. I wish the internet had been available when we started out, because it would have freed us to do—meet—connect," muses Renée.

> We never had any contracts with 99 Records. It was a big financial screw-over. We were just young kids from the Bronx happy to make a record with Factory when they asked us. They paid for the recording time with the producer, Martin Hannett, and they were first to release our three-song EP. We were never signed with anyone; that is one of the reasons I have always been free to release my material. The record was just put out—no accounting, no legal permission, nothing! There was no record contract with ESG's signature on it, with either Factory or 99 Records.

Young Renée's naïveté was permanently punctured when she walked into 99 Records' Bleecker Street store one day—and they asked if she wanted to buy her own ESG EP as a Factory Records UK import. She had not even known the disc existed.

The Scroggins sisters also lost out financially in the collapse of Bahlman's 99 Records, supposedly because of its famous extended lawsuit with Sylvia Robinson's Sugar Hill label over the unlawful sampling of another 99 band, Liquid Liquid, on Grandmaster Flash and the Furious Five's 1984 rap hit, "White Lines (Don't Do It)." "But it was all a lie!" exclaims Renée, aghast at the financial irresponsibility that had enmeshed them. The case had never been filed. "Although I learned a lot about the music business from that experience, it was still a harsh lesson! I try not to dwell on that time," concludes Renée pragmatically.

Now she plays with daughter Nicola and son Nicholas. Renée speaks on the eve of ESG's fortieth anniversary tour, which she says will be her last—though she will still record. "We continue to make music and loops, though now we own it ourselves, which is really cool. I always tell young artists, the music business is a *business* and they should take a business course."

Hard won wisdom. The fiscal abuse ESG experienced along the way with unacknowledged homages from many rappers—the whosampled.com website lists no fewer than 480 ESG samples, including usage by such giants as J. Dilla and the Notorious B.I.G.—prompted these pioneers to name their 1992 12-inch EP *Sample Credits Don't Pay Our Bills*. Appropriately, it features a version of their "Earn It"—one of three cut by the band. Like "Moody," "Earn It" demonstrates how much funk ESG can make with so little—just a square, steady bass figure with a subtle minor twist that drops to a quick pulse, which first falls behind the clattering, top-heavy drums, then pulls ahead of it as Renée's strict, sincere voice repeats:

There ain't nothing in this life is free,
If you want some of that green money

You have to do something called work, you see,
You gotta earn it

"That was the big life lesson from my mom to me. She raised six kids—alone, some of the time. She would say, 'Renée, you can do anything. You gotta have drive and believe in yourself. If you want something, you got to go out and get it.' No one's ever handed me something on a platter. Never let anyone disrespect you—that is the whole key. If you have to walk away, do it," states Renée, echoing her mother with clarity. "It's not worth your dignity. Now I pick and choose."

* * *

That power to choose is itself a victory. Self-taught, no wo/mentors, ESG evolved a unique, minimalist funk palette that proved prophetic, all in isolation. Like Shonen Knife (Boy Knife) from Osaka, Japan, their sound is unmistakable. Both bands share quite different stripped-down sounds—and both consist of sisters. Their two universes spin in the symbiotic dynamic tension of aesthetic opposition. The gritty city throbs within ESG, implying car horns and sirens; Shonen Knife frolic in a pastel wonderland of unpretentious whimsy. Another Bronx/Osaka mirror image: while ESG's mother bought them instruments, seeing music as an escape from the projects, Yamano *mère* didn't like it when her daughter Naoko walked around the house with her guitar. But as the acclaim came, she got the positives, particularly as family has clearly been crucial to the group's longevity. Both sisters are mothers and, Naoko Yamano says, taking children on a rock 'n' roll tour can be challenging. "In our case, we manage by ourselves but it's still difficult. Doing a band with my sister, though, is easy because when we are on the road, we share a hotel room and I can be relaxed with her."

Yet within Shonen Knife's demurely playful demeanor also lurks a streak of city practicality. After the digital deluge of the

1990s, amid the global fight for musicians to reinstate their former income streams via new means, the then ten-year-old group of singer-guitarist Naoko and her drummer sister Atsuko Yamano, with friend Michie Nakatani on bass, delivered a lesson in eco-frugality on 1992's "New Find."

It started with a simple realization. "When I washed my socks, turning them inside out, they became very clean. I was thinking that turning them inside out before washing is a 'new find' for me. I was inspired to write this song. I expanded the main theme, 'new find,' and made lyrics. When I thought about it, I created many examples of 'new find.' There is no relationship between buying new clothes and this song. Anyway, I get happy when I have a 'new find,'" reports Naoko. Their Zen approach, being happy with life's little joys, shines in the innocent open chords and major melodies that ring like a nursery rhyme: small discoveries and appreciations are treats in one's day that can make a person happier, and thus more likely to attract positive interactions.

> Feel in your pockets for something fun
> Wash your socks and turn them inside out
> Try to look hip in old ugly clothes
> There'll be something different in your life
> It's a new find, it's a new find
> It's a new find, it's a new . . .

Sung in English, Shonen Knife's playfulness was a refined response to the all-male Japanese punk scene, which kicked off enthusiastically as soon as the shouts from London and New York hit Tokyo—and Osaka. Their inspiration has encouraged contemporaries like Seagull Screaming Kiss Her Kiss Her and early-twenty-first-century fellow Osaka-dwellers Otoboke Beaver.

"Compared to western punks who arose in opposition to oppressive class structures and stultifying record industries, Shonen Knife's rebellion was against Japan's rigid gender system," notes journalist Daniel Grunebaum, who writes on and promotes Japanese music.

The thought of young women wielding guitars and writing their own songs was practically unheard of in 1980s Japan, where exploitative "agencies" ruled the music business, as they still do. Shonen Knife's revolution was simply to express themselves with unfettered joy—and like their musical lodestone, the Ramones, they did so with an irresistible zest that launched a thousand women rock bands into the wilds of Japan's underground "live house" scene. Shonen Knife didn't rail against the Man—they wrote kooky songs about food—and it's difficult to imagine them seeing themselves as rebelling against anything. Their revolution was in what they did, not what they said.

Western indie rockers like Sonic Youth seized on Shonen Knife and their perma-teen persona, presented in matching pop art gear made by Atsuko. "I've never made our image intentionally; I like to wear a uniform onstage. It's entertainment," says Naoko. They projected girly fantasy with faux-naif songs whose simplicity triggers a little tapped pleasure zone.

"The main stream of everything in Japan is Tokyo, but we are from Osaka, which is very independent. I think the values in Western Japan are different from Eastern Japan. We are special and unique. People in Osaka tend to be unpretentious and friendly. Contents are more important than the surface for people in Osaka," explains Naoko.

* * *

Shonen Knife's sense of jollity combined with that realistic Osaka perspective does also help when one's situation is vulnerable. As first-wave punks were predictably falling off the bottom end of the economic ladder, single girls were likely to plumb new sink-holes of poverty and the risky necessities for survival they may bring. Ingenuity was essential. "Shoplifting," from the Slits' 1979 album *Cut*, vividly depicts a scenario doubtless familiar to at least some of the extended tribe: going into the shops as a posse and doing the old divert-the-shopkeeper's-attention trick, which worked better in those days before CCTV surveillance cameras. Of course, there are rationalizations, none better than those sung by Ari Up: "Babylon won't miss very much / And we'll have supper tonight."

English slang for making a quick getaway before you get caught—"Do a runner!"—is the shouted unison chorus of "Shoplifting." For Slits bassist Tessa Pollitt, the lines also held another meaning: "It happened to my daughter's father, the amazing bass player Sean Oliver of Rip, Rig and Panic (with Neneh Cherry) and to my good friend Jennie Matthias from the group the Belle Stars. Anyone that was black or mixed race in those times was constantly being racially attacked in the streets. It was fight or flight, a matter of survival. If it wasn't racists, it was the police. A single person could be attacked by a mob. Provocative, violent times—you needed to be quick on your feet. . . . Do a runner, Do a runner . . . !!!"

Welcome to the seedy underbelly of postcolonial British culture. The other side of capitalism's coin, though, the lure, is the idea that fun/happiness/contentment/fulfillment can only be enjoyed with money and there's no joy without. Everyone needs to keep the lights on, of course, and they must be bright; but too much caution can stop people taking chances. After all, when is "enough" too little, or when does "little" suffice? Those queens of ducking and diving, the Slits, pose those questions in "Spend, Spend, Spend."

They really were the prototypical girls. The Slits were the originators, where girl punk directly began, and their "Typical Girls" became a seminal anthem. Seeing the Slits play even inspired fellow pioneers the Raincoats—and this writer, for whom the intense group became a surrogate musical family. In their stinky, cat-smelling, deathtrap basement rehearsal room, I wrote about them in 1976 for *Sounds*, when Ari Up was fourteen and they were first forming, was there when they amazed audiences with their random brilliance at New York's Webster Hall; Slit-to-be Neneh Cherry was working a stall in the lobby, selling Slits buttons for punk marketing guerillas Better Badges. We watched with awe as Sun Ra paraded down the aisle of a tiny, rickety theatre, with the electro-magnetic voice of June Tyson leading the way, singing *Space Is the Place*. Such was the freewheeling tribalism of the Slits, that they blithely dynamited the fourth wall between journalist and subject and hauled me over it, calling me to jump on stage with them in venues from a 1970s pre-trendy Glastonbury to obscure, far-flung outposts of pre-gentrification 1990s Brooklyn.

With the scratchy, atonal guitar emblematic of post-punk, and drenched in the spaciness and mystery of Jamaican dub, their sound epitomized that "Punky Reggae" moment. As guitarist Viviane Albertine, who continued to record strong music, recalls in her memoir *Clothes, Clothes, Clothes, Music, Music, Music, Boys, Boys, Boys*, she was first taught to play by then boyfriend Mick Jones of the Clash; they and the Sex Pistols were both friends of the Slits. Their early manager, friend and videographer Don Letts, likes to recount how when the Slits went on the road with the Clash, they were so noisy and unusual—for girls—that the alarmed bus driver was prone to set off without them. The trio all had strong personalities and their own followings. Tessa Pollitt was the moody, sultry bass player, stolid on stage as she kept the groove rolling no matter how wild the top end was. Viv Albertine was the blonde, the most girly of the three, with her tutus and bows. She developed an influential guitar sound, delicate and oblique yet biting—and also wrote the lyrics for "Spend, Spend, Spend."

Unusually highly arranged for a Slits song, the *bierkeller* choruses of "Spend, Spend, Spend" evoke the prewar Berlin music of Kurt Weill, maybe as an ancestral throwback to the crooner father Ari Up barely knew, Frank Forster. The dub vision of producer Dennis Bovell, however, makes each element of the minimalist sound ring in dynamic tension. Budgie (later of Siouxsie and the Banshees) plays drums that are abrupt, unexpected—a heartbeat that trips, then persists. Albertine's guitar, always jagged, stings like electric shocks of anxiety, sometimes doubling Up's heedless warble that free-forms conversationally over Pollitt's determined bass. Breathless as if she were running away from Babylon, Up spins into her own spiral of fascinated fear at her own urges. As she enters the chorus, her voice drops low and confidential, like a junkie in a strange town asking someone in a bar where they can score:

> I want to buy
> (Have you been affected?)
> I need consoling
> (You could be addicted)
> I need something new . . .
> I want to satisfy this empty feeling

"Part of it is being so very poor, being an outsider looking in. The video that Don Letts made shows how I used to look into windows and try and learn how other people lived. Middle-class people. It was another world," Albertine reflects. "I especially couldn't believe that they were comfortable with not drawing their curtains, so anyone passing by could see what they were doing and wearing, and how they were behaving. My family was too violent and poor to let anyone see any of that."

Albertine's background was quite different from Ari Up's; although she always sided with the ragamuffins and sufferers, Up was a second-generation dropout from a wealthy German publishing family. A feral wild child, she began loudly growing up on stage. Her stylish German mother, Nora, was a "face" in generations of the London pop scene, briefly promoting Jimi Hendrix. (She later married John Lydon, thus making the Sex Pistol and Public Image Limited founder Up's stepfather.)

Punky hip-hop-electro-jazz artiste Neneh Cherry, part of the Slits in the late 1970s, was raised harmolodically, in the free-flowing style pioneered by her trumpeter stepfather, Don Cherry, who played with Ornette Coleman. Neneh and Ari Up became instant *sistr'en* (Jamaican patois for "sisterfriends"), both performing—and having children—young. Neneh says, "I realize now that I would hear them on a deeper level, because the Slits were avant-garde. I would feel my own upbringing in their music. They were a big part of my journey."

For Up, the voyage was always tempestuous. "All my life I have felt trapped, fighting for my freedom," she said fiercely when I interviewed her for the band's final album, *Trapped Animal*, in 2009.

With her huge blue eyes and pineapple cluster of dreads, Up was full-on and charismatic as she dodged Babylon and society's "traps" of convention. At Jah Shaka's thunderous dub reggae sound system dances in the 1970s, all the serious dreads would be amazed at Up's heavy martial "stepping," the athletic, *capoeira*-style dance of the day. Her remarkable arc included time spent living with her children in the jungles of Belize ("amazing, free-spirit people," she described), and in Kingston's edgy Waterhouse area as "Madusa," a dancehall queen. Less than a year after the death of Poly Styrene from breast cancer, Ari Up also succumbed to the disease in 2010, a double blow for the She-Punk movement.

Helping form the Slits was Up's first attempt at escaping the trap. Nora was an early den mother to the band. Tessa Pollitt was eighteen, moving from squat to squat. One had no plumbing, causing her to "use the pub next door if it was open, or just [not] eat too much." She says, "If I was really hungry, I would get up early, and if a house had more than one milk bottle on the doorstep, I didn't think they would miss one—maybe the milkman forgot to deliver! Sometimes a pint of milk is as good a meal as a steak!"

Up was still living at home and Pollitt often took shelter there; Nora fed her and bought her first bass from Sex Pistols guitarist Steve Jones. Pollitt also enjoyed sharing a squat with Palmolive, a Spanish girl who became the Slits' first drummer and a lyricist too; she was fresh from living in yet another squat in Shepherd's Bush with her then boyfriend Joe Strummer, later of the Clash, who was known as Woody.

"Many people from my generation left home young, and it was not hard to find a dis-used property to make a temporary home for a reasonable length of time. It is not so easy nowadays, hence the rising number of homeless," notes Pollitt.

Then as now, for the majority it could seem almost impossible to escape from the cycle of poverty and debt—though the hope was always there and kept one going. Some who found a way to bust out, even if their doings were dodgy, would be admired and envied by some of those left behind, stuck in the same old rut. Hence the late period Sex Pistols' flirtation in Brazil with refugee outlaw Ronnie Biggs, the infamous Great Train Robber; and, rather differently, Viv Albertine's fascination with an older blonde who seemed to have beaten the system, even though she would soon blow it all. Albertine's fellow Viv, Viv Nicholson, had had four children and two marriages by the time husband number two won £152,319 in 1961 on the football pools.

On the way to collect the check, Viv Nicholson said to reporters the classic line that Viv Albertine took as a title. Even while she was boasting about her imminent orgy of spending, Nicholson was wearing stockings she had been forced to borrow from her sister. As if in compensation for Nicholson's poor, hungry childhood spent caring for sick family members, the couple's heedless extravagance became a national scandal—and cause for envy. But like Icarus in the Greek myths, it all came tumbling down, and Nicholson's fulfilled dreams would destroy her. Soon after their big score, her husband died in an accident. Still, nothing was ever enough for Nicholson. Burning through the remaining cash, she rapidly found herself broker than before. Flawed and cautionary though the tale was, more than their coincidence of names drew Albertine to write the song.

"I was about twelve when it happened. She was famous for fifteen minutes, but she made a huge impression on me. Ebullient and quick witted. In the newspapers, she was considered outrageous and shocking to be so outspoken and frivolous and not saying something like 'I'm going to buy my mother a house.' It was so hard to find role models and inspirational irreverent women in those days. I clung on to anyone who showed some *chutzpah*," says Albertine.

"Very early on, spending money, buying things, became a way for me to comfort myself (self soothe), but I also was ashamed of this and the whole acquisitive nature of capitalism, which I was sort of poking fun at and highlighting in the song," she continues. 'Spend, Spend, Spend' was written in the mid-late 1970s, when capitalism was still a newish concept to the UK working classes. Thatcher [was] just about to come into power in 1979 and set us down that road we are still very much traveling along and committed to."

* * *

Viv Albertine is describing a societal switch, Davida changing Goliath's gears, as society's political pendulum laboriously swings from left to right and back again in asymmetrical circles. Like the great worm of ancient mythology, Ourobouros, which eats its own tail, the extremes of both supposedly separate "poles" seem really to meet, much of the time. It's as if the earth actually was flat. The Slits' music would become even more spacey and dubby with their next album, *Earthbeat*, before they split for a while and Up headed for Belize, in protest against 1980s materialism as much as anything else. Those unable to register their displeasure so drastically found themselves adjusting to the new stress of fitting in by having *stuff*—expense accounts and Filofaxes and power-dressing, phonebook-size mobile phones, mortgages and designer brands. All of which had suddenly become a vital index of self-worth, though they had just recently been scorned (or didn't exist, in the case of mobile phones). The rightward tilt was not just pushed by Reagan and Thatcher. Gorbachev's glasnost loosening of Russia's constellation of unified states in the late 1980s saw the collapse of traditional Communism. Like China soon after, an exuberant appetite for the long-denied capitalist fruits of consumer and luxury goods was unleashed.

"I am against money; it shouldn't exist," says composer/keyboardist Nastya Mineralova of Moscow's Pussy Riot collective. "So I have to compromise. Music for me is a field extremely free from money. I appreciate its creativity, its organizational aspect: you are doing it only because you really want to do it, not because you want to trade your time as you would for, say, a piece of chocolate," Mineralova continues. "For me, this is the key concept of life, from early childhood: to free your mind from any influences the best you can, to then realize what it is you want to achieve, and to do it. I believe that's the only way to do new things that no one has done before."

She remembers the knock-on effect of Gorbachev's consumerist changes two decades on, under Vladimir Putin. "All through the 2000s, in Russia we had huge salaries, gigantic supermarkets, just like you have in America. We enthusiastically went to Miami and Provence for holidays, ate foreign food, used Paco Rabanne and wore American Apparel," she says. "But as soon as the bell of fashion rang for patriotism and religion—the Russian Orthodox Church—everyone started writing on their Volkswagens and Mercedes, "Trophy from Berlin"—as if their expensive modern cars were spoils of war from the Red Army's triumphant taking of Berlin in 1945."

When his Russian rule began with the new century, part of Putin's mission, along with sweeping away the previous crew of corrupt oligarchs, was backpedaling on glasnost and edging towards the reunification of Russia. His strategy included summoning the old Russian nationalist soul by reinforcing the links between church and state that had been verboten under Communism. Increasingly, the Russian Orthodox Church reemerged as a political force, and with it, views on women's reproductive rights so reductive as to seem barbaric to progressives in the rich world. For free-thinking women, such as the members of Pussy Riot, the bonhomie between Putin and the head of the church for Moscow and all of Russia, His Holiness Patriarch Kirill, was truly an unholy alliance.

Moscow Cathedral proved to be the stage for the action that shot the band into international attention: a brilliantly executed guerilla flash performance of their song "A Punk Prayer" in 2012. Two Pussy Riot members, Nadya Tolokonnikova and Maria "Masha" Alyokhia, were sent to distant, brutal jails. Associated with other Moscow guerilla arts movements prior to their shocking incarceration, the band had already been making art actions not only in clubs but, in the Situationist spirit, wherever they might disrupt the regular flow of whatever they were against. That could be religion, as in "A Punk Prayer," protesting Putin's work with Patriarch Kirill to withdraw women's reproductive rights, or as shown in the video for "Kropotkin Vodka," the hypocrisy and avid embrace of consumerism that had been propelling Russia's elite after Communism—and the role of a mythical brand of vodka in helping bring about new revolution:

Occupy the city with a kitchen frying pan
Hang out with a vacuum cleaner, get off with it,
Seduce battalions of police damsels
Naked cops rejoice in the new reforms

The fucking end to sexist conformists!
The fucking end to sexist Putinists!

After the testing experience of incarceration and the global head-lines that followed, Alyokhia created a theatrical piece called "Revolution": not so much a musical, more an audiovisual multimedia narrative musical performance. The small cast of players included two members of the band AWOTT, whose keyboard player Nastya Mineralova was also in Pussy Riot. A longtime associate of the band confided, "As far as making the actual music goes, talk to Nastya." Onstage, she was a strong presence in a complex and emotional show.

Told with pungent economy, the chilling performance hurtles along, evoking how and why the band became a focus for feminist outrage and protest. In an experience rather different from that of many in this book, artists from Russia and Eastern Europe often spend more time battling the dominant system as a whole, alongside the men, rather than sexism. "I think to be divided by gender is boring. Pussy Riot members were not only women, and no one checked the gender of potential members. Pussy Riot is a prank on orthodox feminists and a result of a friendship of two people, as it commonly happens. To be honest, I don't think punk has anything to do with it. Woman is free when she doesn't need a man as a reason and center of her existence," says Mineralova, explaining that despite the issues still facing Russian women, feminism had been known, and women had worked alongside men, since the 1917 revolution. "Women would give birth to children and come back to work in just a few days. Didn't matter if they were working at a factory or in the theatre."

Russian journalist Xenia Grubstein, associate producer of the 2013 Pussy Riot documentary *A Punk Prayer*, helped me communicate with the band (and with Fértil Miseria from Colombia). She notes, "We have to be very careful in tough times because they get used by the patriarchy to push their agenda, while everyone is busy fighting amongst themselves. But in my experience, men and women unite when they face a bigger evil and put aside their differences because the goal is to fight, and win." She continues, "Personally, ever since I was very little, I remember a sort of confusion about subscribing to a gender identity, because first and foremost I felt like a person with my own ambitions and aspirations."

Mineralova is of the same mind. "I don't think about myself as a woman that much. I grew up with my mother without fathers or stepfathers. I don't have a pattern of woman-man behavior. Before I thought it was hindering me, but then realized, as an absence of any stereotype, it's hugely liberating," she says.

Don't knock the original Spice Girls for being 1990s fake fronts for a bunch of manipulative, fantasizing male producers. Their ersatz "Girl Power!" slogan, cribbed from Kathleen Hanna and Riot Grrrls, touched Mineralova's generation in Russia with no cynicism attached. The Beatles first moved her, then the Spice Girls, and Sonic Youth and the Pixies gave Mineralova a musical home. Before keyboards, she played bass, inspired by Sonic Youth's Kim Gordon and the Breeders' Kim Deal. Of emotional free-jazz keyboard player Annette Peacock, Mineralova says, "When I saw her frowny smile on the sleeve of her LP *Back to the Beginning*, I understood that women have a right to be shy."

The mythical liquor which songwriters Nadya Tolokonnikova and Katya Samutsevitch invoke to help empower weak people to fight for change, much as Popeye supersizes when he downs spinach, is named after Piotr Kropotkin (1842–1921). A dropout from both the military and his aristocratic family who chose cooperation over competition, he was one of the founders of the anarchism that motivated Vi Subversa and Crass. "Kropotkin Vodka is a drink that moves people to protest, burn, and destroy," says Mineralova.

She had no formal musical education, but Mineralova's talent lies behind the accessibility of "Kropotkin Vodka." From the start, the frenetic track takes and shakes the listener in its great jaws of fuzzy guitars and drums. The anonymous vocalist—all Pussy Rioters would remain unknown, ideally, hence the famous balaclavas concealing their features—barks out lyrics like a slap in Babylon's face. Sirens wail as the track builds to a climax shouted in unison. The frenzied song is structured so that if the track has to be stopped abruptly, it will still make sense—like if the show is broken up by the police, as happens in the video—working in part because the song structure is arranged as neat and tight as the surfing 45 it distantly resembles, but on heavy Ritalin.

"By the time we made 'Kropotkin Vodka' in 2012, me and Maxim Ionov from AWOTT had been doing music together for about six years. I made a cool beat with a Korg synthesizer and added bass. Maxim helped with keyboards—a tender, electrifying melody. I'm grateful to him for that. I barely knew how to make cool tunes and I wanted to," says Mineralova. "For a Russian person in the 2000s to 2010s, punk was still something exotic and artificial, a collection of stereotypes. But maybe it's the same thing there in your West when artists come in to play? Nadja and Katya wanted something more vintage, they needed a guitar. I liked Atari Teenage Riot, who seemed like the coolest, loudest, most rebellious sound, with the minimum of instruments. Lots of lyrics, loud beats, synthesizers that cut your ears. Voice and sampler, I thought. That's the minimalistic direction Pussy Riot need to be heading in to perform on the street."

Mineralova's recipe for the Pussy Riot sound is tested and wins in the urban action of "Kropotkin Vodka," shot on video by enthusiastic activists. "There was nothing arranged, no film set," says Mineralova. "No one knew how to play guitar either." In the video, dressed in their trademark graphic outlines in primary colors with bright balaclavas, Pussy Riot belt the tune, spray a fire extinguisher at the elated crowd, use all of the impromptu stage they can, and grab every second till the surprise event is forced to stop—as it inevitably will be. The riotous agit-gig is intercut with the balaclava-clad girls in their garish quick-getaway gear, savaging consumerism by pogoing amid the sleek white and gold of a posh boutique stuffed with handbags worth thousands—the new luxury gods of the Russian elite that have replaced the old leaders.

"I don't separate women into a special human category, neither do I separate punk from music in general. The current divide is outdated, don't you think?" Mineralova concludes. "I think we should blend them all together, and then divide them anew into entities that are more contemporary—all the music styles, genders, all forms of art, religions, and also all the money of the world. Shopping is something we do when we come across some money to compensate for our own lack of joy of living. As a punk, I want to achieve an extreme not out of love, but out of boredom."

* * *

In post-Communist Russia, in post-punk New York, even in comparatively staid Hastings on England's scenic south coast, the deadly feeling that the Roman Stoic philosopher Lucius Seneca called *tedium*—a great lassitude and lack of interest in anything, which Mineralova calls boredom—has been touted as a passive engine of punk. However, here's the flip side of the 45: it's all still the same record. Listen beyond the words. Un-boredom pumps from both Pussy Riot and Maid of Ace's 2016 "Made in England." The high and rising riff of the latter's twanged guitar as it giddily hops between chords screams, "Optimism! Tomorrow!"—a defiant taunt to an increasingly corporatized global elite that seeks to overturn even the regional authority and autonomous national interests of the governments that punks so often have reason to criticize.

Maid of Ace are siblings. All conforming to the ACE acronym—singer-songwriter Alison "Ali" Cara, guitarist Anna Coral, drummer Abby Charlotte, and bassist Amy Catherine—the Elliott sisters are a genetic gang of four.

Despite the hectic hurtle of "Made in England," which bashes along as cheery and direct as the football stadium anthem it may yet become, the song is nonetheless as nostalgic as Dame Vera Lynn's wartime hit "White Cliffs of Dover." After her 2015 marriage to the singer of Los Angeles punk band A Pretty Mess, Ali began shuttling between Hastings and his home; this paean to Britishness was made in Los Angeles.

"This song started due to homesickness, and also relates to wanting to be on the road. You're stuck in your shit hole of a town and you just want to get out—then you're out and you just want to come home. It's a bittersweet circle!" laughs Ali.

They careen about their "manor" (neighborhood) on bicycles in the video for the title track of their first album, *Maid in England* (2016), just like their contemporaries Skinny Girl Diet; but while SGD are supergirl vinyl avengers saving distraught women from vile fates, the happily populist Maid of Ace wind up down in their local pub, hanging out with their mates and having a beer, smoking a spliff on the seafront, drinking from beer cans and cider bottles on the playground swings. Shot at their actual "local," the video suggests how these good citizens of Hastings are responding to the Situationist challenges set out by Guy Debord, who questioned the validity of people spending their time in the sort of soul-destroying jobs that Maid of Ace's generation can hardly find anyway.

"Us and most of our friends work in pubs or are on the dole [welfare]! That's standard in Hastings! You are in and out of jobs all the time. We've probably worked in half the pubs in that town!" says Ali.

Interestingly, the only jobs that Maid of Ace can imagine working alongside music are those involved in panaceas, specifically booze to deaden or alleviate that "boredom" which Mineralova describes. But the signal sent by the all-ages people in the pub, none of them dentally implanted Hollywood types, is that they are enjoying life (at least for that moment). Hard as it may be for alienated digerati to believe, the non-actors in the Maid of Aces video, the band's real-life friends, genuinely do appreciate the face-to-face closeness of their own un-virtual community. And it is this rootsy, unpretentious connection that costs nothing—OK, maybe a round of beer in this instance, though alternative stimulants could also work—which can keep people effective, even happy, when the "normal" societal supports are under attack. Maid of Ace sing about England, but their songs can apply to wherever you are. With their enthusiastic voices, surging rhythm attack, and organic populist choruses, Maid of Ace are tacticians who show us how to keep going.

Pressure to conform in a highly structured, competitive working environment is not always conducive to art (decades of legendary UK music scenes were made possible by the creative time available to art students), and the girls know it. This is not their only song about money. Ali wrote "Raise the Minimum Wage" when she was in some soul-sucker gig where she hoped to get promoted so she could actually start to get the minimum wage. Then she hoped it would get raised. Many will relate to its opener, as Ali growls, "I go to my bank every day / And it says the same thing / (digitized voice) You have zero pounds and zero pence."

"Hastings has a lot of artistic and musical talent, and I think a lot of that has to do with the way of life there. We work enough to just about scrape by, because doing what we love is more important than having a steady 9 to 5 job and a big pay check," she comments. "Also, it's a lot harder to find/get those types of jobs anyway. There's definitely a lot of duckin' and divin' where we're from! I don't know how people afford to live; half the time we're still squatting—at our Mum's house! Haha!"

Mother says to get a job,
I'm drinking Strongbow (cider) in the pub,
Stuck in a rut, I'm not giving up
I've seen the world, but when I've had enough,
Everywhere we roam, all roads lead to home . . .
'Cos we're made in England, We're made in England . . .

Clearly still jobless, in the video Maid of Ace slope out of the Job Centre, giggling—they can still crash at home, much as Tessa

Pollitt stayed with den mother Nora. "We managed on no cash," Pollitt remembered. "I did not want or know how to do a normal job. We wanted to put 100 percent time, energy, and dedication into the Slits; we were on a mission." Unemployment was high, strikes were stopping basic services, public morale was low, and jobs were super scarce when the scuffling Slits yearned for material goods outside shop windows. At the same time, New York, with its homeless tent cities and burned-out tenements, was a city dismissed as unsalvageable by the federal government and collapsing into the crack and AIDS epidemics. The Bush Tetras' Cynthia Sley told *The Guardian*, "No one worked. Everyone was just doing music or art or film or theatre or some crazy thing: a lot of people with a lot of ideas happening at once. I didn't really know anyone who worked. And that does not happen at all now." In other words, Pollitt and Sley would have not wanted a straight job, even if they could have got one. Still, they wanted some people to have work, if only so they would have a paying audience. Maybe not for artists, but for most people, conventional jobs represent both income and self-respect.

Back then, in both England and America, the expectation was that at some point, employment would return. The situation of the generation that Maid of Ace represent differs in that there are very few and will be fewer jobs for regular folk without high-level digital skills. Automation, digitization, corporatization, and globalization plus companies like Amazon and Google—virtually nations themselves that can threaten real governments—challenge the small, local independent entrepreneur. The widening, engineered chasm between the nearly all-male 1 percent that holds half the world's wealth and the rest of us threatens. So Maid of Ace work in the pub when they are not touring because they can't pull off what Pollitt and Sley did in the wilder, freer 1970s; and they work in pubs because apart from anything else, so much of the High Street has closed while the pleasure palaces of the pubs remain. Besides, the band rehearses upstairs. They are the bards of the post-work generation, for whom the wealth divide has become so vast that an uneducated underclass is created and left to fend for itself. They will have to duck and dive—and find a way to not be bored. In the vibrancy of Maid of Ace's song, with its innate spirit of resistance, lies some solution.

As this chapter was being written, women at Britain's BBC, like their counterparts in the Hollywood movie industry, were vehemently protesting the ever-increasing size of the deliberately hidden pay gap between themselves and their male co-workers. When I mentioned it to an independent media professional girl-friend, she replied, "So what's new?" Sometimes it seems as if equal pay for women is such a long-standing cause that it lacks the glamor of "newer" issues. Some artists in this book were loath to define themselves as "feminist." However, ask if they believe in equal pay for women, and they always do—which means they are feminists, after all.

The insanely extended struggle for women's equal pay may be invisible simply because of its age—ironically, the fate that many women fear. The gender pay gap is a wound that will make society unequal until it is fixed. Look at it all in the context of the 2010s and beyond: it is unlikely that the future will suddenly see an upsurge in the sort of jobs non-specialists can do in the age of drones and driverless cars. Against this backdrop, set the con-tinuing financial devaluation of the arts, on the humble cultural worker level anyway. Further, factor in the under-appreciation of female input generally, as proven by the shattered, scattered herstory of women in punk music itself. Mix it up by locating all these ingredients within the same mega-corporate societies that leave the individual with ever less space and more surveil-lance, and few chances to crack the big success/comfort piñata; it dangles so tantalizingly over our heads even as the bough from which it hangs, held by the controlling 1 percent, is raised higher and higher.

And yet Maid of Ace and their mates in the pub still want us to see that they are undefeated. They still have a good time, because they are fired by the same cheery, confrontational energy that they project in their music: the feisty survivalist feeling that ensures every underdog has its day. Happiness makes strength. Against all odds, the Elliott sisters are really singing, "We will find a way to stick it to the Man by living and playing how we want."

The audacity and courage of female artists who defy the odds is to be celebrated; like the women in this chapter, who find a way to dig life and create what they want *with or without money* by combining whatever resources they have. And when Babylon and/or the universe does decide to lavish its fruits on you, don't swallow it all up for yourself. Keep more than solvent to do what you need to do—but don't forget to also spread it around. Just like Patti Smith did.

LINEUP & TRACK LISTING

1. Crass, "Smother Love" (UK, 1981).
From the anarcho-punk collective's female liberation LP Penis Envy. Savage satire of marriage over thunderous drums.

2. Cherry Vanilla, "The Punk" (US, 1977).
Glam Warhol/Bowie scenemaker Cherry Vanilla's pure love for UK punk shines through.

3. Gia Wang/Hang on the Box, "Asshole, I'm Not Your Baby" (China, 2001).
Fiery unlove song by China's first all-girl punk band, who don't want to be controlled by boyfriends.

4. Vivien Goldman, "Launderette" (UK, 1981).
Yes, this book's author is also a post-punk singer-songwriter who enjoyed a surprise revival decades later. Here's my trenchant take on an unlove encounter.

5. Chrissie Hynde, "Precious" (UK/US, 1979).
Chemistry sizzles between the edgy girl and the bad boy. Will she play it safe? From a punk with a timeless voice.

6. Kartika Jahja/Tika & the Dissidents, "Tubuhku Otoritasku" ("My Body, My Choice") (Indonesia, 2016).
Bold indictment of sex crimes and claiming of female rights from a punk confronting a repressive regime.

7. 7 Year Bitch, "M.I.A." (US, 1994).
Rage and pain at the rape and murder of their friend and mentor, singer Mia Zapata, inspired this Seattle band to make more visceral music.

8. Rhoda Dakar with the Special AKA, "The Boiler" (UK, 1982).
Cinematic, harrowing extended narrative song of date rape from a leading lady of the 2 Tone ska movement.

9. Alice Bag/the Bags, "Babylonian Gorgon" (US, 1990).
Is she dissing a lover or the patriarchy? LA's Alice Bag uses a mix of mythologies to put him/it down.

10. Grace Jones, "My Jamaican Guy" (Jamaica/US 1982).
The inimitable, beyond-genre Grace Jones comes to terms with her roots in this hypnotic love/lust song.

11. Tribe 8, "Check Out Your Babe" (US, 1996).
San Francisco's playful but pungent dyke tribe bring new possibilities to the dance floor. Boys, lock up your girlfriends!

12. The Au Pairs, "It's Obvious" (UK, 1981).
Committed, engaged, and rather ironic, the activist Au Pairs project a mating game where gender equality rules.

13. The Mo-Dettes, "White Mice" (UK, 1979).
The saucy Mo-Dettes hug girly frivolity. They decide when they feel like flirting—and who the lucky feller will be.

14. Neneh Cherry, "Buffalo Stance" (UK/Sweden, 1988).
Cosmopolitan avant-gardist Neneh Cherry's track dazzles with its complex depiction of street charisma seduction.

3

LOVE/UNLOVE

Busting Up the Binary

The word "mourns" might get attached to other emotion words: anger, hate, love. The replacement of one word for an emotion with another word produces a narrative. Our love might create the condition for our grief, our loss could become the condition for our hate, and so on.

Sara Ahmed, *Cultural Politics of Emotion*, 2004

"I'M NOT SURE WHAT you mean by 'why'? Why anything?" artist Gee Vaucher, co-founder of British proto-anarcho-punks Crass and lyricist of their "Smother Love," responded to a query about the song—thus proving that the myth of the band known for questioning everything was real. A devastating dissection of the hypocritical pap used to peddle marriage, its jet energy and scathing verse rained down on the patriarchy like boiling oil poured from castle battlements. Crass spit on marriage as a one-sided microsystem of societal control.

Always dressed in black, they resided communally in Britain's rural Dial House, Essex. The sixteenth-century cottage had an open-door policy and could be considered the nonhierarchical anti-Camelot. Jamaican Rastas refer to the capitalist/neoconservative or neoliberal social system as Babylon, and Crass agree with them that the old approach is exploitative and ripe for collapse. Both abhor and reject its fruits. (When David Bowie rejected the Queen's knighthood and told no one—now, that was punk.)

So why love? Why not love? Punk is often associated with war and hate—but only because it followed the seeming crash of 1960s hippy ideals. It masqueraded under another name, but the ultimate goals were the same, just in mirror writing. After all, when Crass first began in 1977, some of the founders did mate and continued to relate for at least the seven years of the band's existence. So, no matter how detached or cynical one may be about the romantic projections of love fed to us by consumerism, love will and does persist, wiggling through fissures in the hardest emotional armor. Love seems nonnegotiable, like air or water. A series of high-profile scandals erupted in the 2010s, from the serial accusers of everyone's uncle, Bill Cosby, to the kickoff of the #MeToo movement with Harvey Weinstein's fall from the peak of filmic near-absolute power. Naturally, the ever-predatory music industry had its suddenly redundant idols. Producer Dr. Luke was sued by punky singer Ke$ha for sexual harassment before the #MeToo movement of 2016 opened the floodgates of male-privilege-abuse shame, drowning the reputations of figures like producer/industry titan L. A. Reid and even the radical zen hip-hop guru Russell Simmons. The old *Cosmopolitan* magazine way of having to sleep with a much older producer to ensure a record deal is really un-punk (unless you are sure you really, really dig him, of course; that is different). To do what you have to do, sometimes one might even choose to go without, get out of the romance gear to prevent dangerous cracks in the road through which a girl's own power can seep. That is, until the moment, the person, is right. And punk love often seems to be about mistakes made along the way to that elusive quasi-destination. The reckless abandon of punk can often lead to unpredictable passions and, for vulnerable girls, healthy self-love can get lost in the beat. Equally, those wild times may be great fuel for nostalgic future reveries.

Anyway, when punk began in the mid-1970s, it was an invigorating yet confusing time for sexuality. Love songs were perceived in the counterculture as being a bit weedy and wet; unlove songs were the way to go. Then governor of California, Ronald Reagan, signed into effect America's first no-fault divorce law in 1970. According to a 2011 report by the census bureau, divorce rates then continued to rise steadily, surging in the early 1990s, just in time to coincide with Riot Grrrl. The brief and, for many, glorious window for rampant sexuality that opened with the advent of penicillin and the pill was, in England and New York, quite un-puritanical. Homosexuality had been legalized in Britain in 1967. The horror of being called a "slut" that the Riot Grrrls were to battle in America's Pacific Northwest in the 1990s was not even an issue in Britain, where it was assumed that all punks, boys and girls, were sluts and glad of it.

Why, then, its obverse—unlove? Though often played out onstage by bands like San Francisco's Tribe 8, the further shores of love—what happily "vanilla" people regard as extreme sex like sadomasochism and fetish—were naturally tested. Though norms are seemingly there to be busted, innocent punks were to discover that some taboos really should never be broken; tragically, even pedophilia was a part of punk's saga. Former Sex Pistols manager Malcolm McLaren's nude cover shot of underage singer Annabella Lwin for Bow Wow Wow, the band he assembled, were a hint. The T-shirts of naked prepubescent boys sold by SEX, the King's Road clothing boutique McLaren owned with his then wife, designer Dame Vivienne Westwood, would be regarded as less "cool" today; a deluge of pedophile scandals have hopefully created firmer boundaries against behavioral patterns of institutional abuse of a kind most people would once have scarcely believed could exist. It even destabilized the venerable BBC, virtually the only British medium at the time—with both sexism and pedophilia being rampant when punk began. Tragically, women's unlove saga goes beyond a rattling of antique conventions.

The impish, provocateur spirit of Guy Debord's Situationist philosophy underpinned the events that would play out around the album on which "Smother Love" appears—*Penis Envy*, its title taken from a 1908 Sigmund Freud work. Among the Crass crew, Freud's approach was viewed with skepticism if not derision for its presumptive missionary position view of sex and, by extension, gender relations. Didn't Freud secretly yearn for breasts on the quiet, just for a change? Dedicated to disemboweling such inequity, *Penis Envy* followed Crass' offering of the previous year, *The Feeding of the 5000*. Their comment on Prime Minister Margaret Thatcher's self-aggrandizing Falklands War articulated the widespread sense that the conflict was more about manipulating a crisis to keep her in office, regardless of lives lost, than defending the interests of the Falkland Islanders, stuck in their corner of colonial struggle. Tricksters, Crass intercut the crystalline upper-middle-class tones of their vocalist, Eve Libertine, imitating Margaret Thatcher with foraged audio of Ronald Reagan and faked a 1981 tape suggesting the two complicit heads of state were actually arguing over the conduct of the Falklands War. Infiltrated via Holland, the forgery fooled enough people to create a frenzy at the highest level; both governments feared mischief by the Kremlin. Notoriety bred sales, and their Thatcher/Reagan commentary called for an equally weighty successor—or whatever Crass thought was interesting at the time, which happened to be sexism.

The significance of the collective's next project, *Penis Envy*, was assured when it was banned and seized as an "Obscene Article for Publication for Gain" from Eastern Bloc, an indie record store in Manchester. Much was the surprise among the staff and readership of *Loving*, a teen magazine that peddled the flummery of romance, at the reaction to their free, white vinyl flexi-disc of an anodyne ballad called "Our Wedding"—it had been offered to them for free by a group called Creative Recording and Sound Services (get it?). Actually, it blasted matrimony as fiercely as anarchist Emma Goldman (1869–1940), who roared, "It is this slavish acquiescence to man's superiority that has kept the marriage institution seemingly intact for so long a period." As later generations would say, *Loving* had been "punked."

If indeed the giveaway lured adolescent girls to delve further, they would have heard a coruscating disembowelment of what Crass saw as the rotting carcass of a corrupt institution, marriage, being pimped by *Loving*. "Smother Love" was like luring the youth with sugary soda, then switching it for raw, green juice. Feminist intellectuals of the 1970s, such as Dale Spender in her book *Man-Made Language*, analyzed how one of the most concise and colorful languages, English, could shape our mentality with such a bias towards people with penises. This thinking was not lost on Crass, who had confounded conventional expectations of anarchism by selling well, almost despite themselves.

"We had just released *The Feeding of the 5000* and were exploring the next project. *Feeding* was a surprisingly successful record and the audience was expecting more of the same, but it wasn't the way we worked. The women in the band had something more to say on the subject of sexism and other 'isms' that hold a person down and contribute to the separation, so we started writing new songs," explains Gee Vaucher. "Ideas percolate. When enough material had been written, then we started recording. It took as long as it took. There was no pressure of a deadline."

Eve Libertine's upper-class clarity and crispness hurled top-speed words like bricks at a demonstration, contrasting with skittering phased guitar on a rhythm that resides somewhere between tribal drums and a military band playing in a park at teatime on an English Sunday afternoon. It makes for a fast and furious feminist one and a half minutes.

> Tell me I'm your everything, let us build a home
> We can build a house for two, with little ones to follow
> The proof of our normality that justifies tomorrow
> Romance, romance . . .
> Love's another skin-trap, another social weapon
> Another way to make men slaves and women at their beckon

The words roll from Libertine's tongue with lubricous precision, evoking whole dramas, sarcasm dripping acid-laced honey from every caressed, pell-mell syllable. The song becomes a carnival ghost ride through the horrors of the depressing politics they perceived as playing out in so many marriages around them, and the pressure for wedlock from the dominant society, rules that had to be obeyed for admittance and approval.

* * *

As punk is a loose collective of different people united in being deemed outsiders by conventional standards—norms which themselves shift like a rope bridge slung between melting icebergs in a high wind—some degree of alienation is the default mode of punk love. Just enough exist to confirm that regular love songs are not usually the punk thing: Seattle band L7's "Till the Wheels Fall Off," Bratmobile's queenly "Come Hither," or the Runaways' "You Drive Me Wild." Doubtless there are others, but starting with no expectations is recommended for punk love—as indeed, some would say, for any attachment. Those with a more structured life are less likely to be drawn to the unruliness of punk (unless it touches something primitive, locked deep within).

In the fairly narrow field of unabashed punk love songs, perhaps the purest is "The Punk" by marketer, writer, actress, and then musician Cherry Vanilla. Much mid- to late-century American culture is shaped by the looming presence of Andy Warhol, whose affinity for transvestites made stars out of personalities like Candy Darling and who provided a focus for cycles of the New York art scene; the Velvet Underground was his house band. Naturally, he took to the archly androgynous glam music coming out of mid-1970s England, in which bisexuality was a virtue. Among the acolytes who connected Warhol with the Glam King, David Bowie, was Cherry Vanilla. The song is from her 1977 *Bad Girls* LP, on which Bowie's trusted spokeswoman sports a little red rooster head of hair that likely came from Manic

Panic's dye chart and makes her look like Ziggy Stardust's fun cousin.

"Well, we never considered ourselves a punk band, but we were monitoring the punk movement in the UK with so much interest . . . plus the Ramones were representing it in the US. So, it's about the UK punks (bless them), the Ramones, and my boyfriend/co-writer at the time, Louie Lepore," recalls Cherry Vanilla. "We felt it was a great little pop song that was catchy and could be played on the radio, and we hoped it was to be our big hit! It wasn't. But now it seems to have a new life of its own. Young bands in Germany and Italy do live versions of it, and that is so thrilling. It lives."

The sort of straight ahead rock 'n' roll band in which a very young Ziggy might have wanted to play guitar rampages around Cherry Vanilla's slightly Jersey Girl vocals as she rolls the smoking words around her tongue:

Black leather jacket and a cycle slut
Big sunglasses and a big haircut
Studs all up and down his faded jeans
Says he's from the city but he comes from Queens
Hot pink guitar and a faded amp
Walks onstage like he is a champ . . .

"The Punk" taps into suburban teen yearning for if not a walk, then at least a cruise through the wild side. Its limpid worship of the bad boys on stage taps into the deepest aspirational stratum of fandom. It is arguably punk's most innocent love song—to itself.

* * *

Punk features more unlove songs than love songs. How could it be otherwise, when it's made by outsiders wrestling with the octopus arms of the patriarchy? It's the loud sound designed to send the old walls tumbling down (and that has also come to refer to not just 1950s dating conventions, but gender). Since punk started in the 1970s, the existing system has always been seen as crumbling—and often with it, expectations of long-lasting domesticity.

All the affection that shimmers through "The Punk" is absent from, and all of Crass' contempt for sentimental consumerist claptrap seems channeled through "Asshole, I'm Not Your Baby" from the *Yellow Banana* album by Hang on the Box, China's first all-girl punk band.

> I don't want another boy
> To tempt me
> I don't want to lie,
> Are you ready to take me with you?
> Asshole, I'm not your baby!

* * *

"You don't want to hear what I have to say," snarls Gia Wang, their singer-songwriter, who made the record in 2001 when she was 18. "I am a bad bitch. I am childish and capricious. Tearing up a man's heart is as easy as tearing a piece of paper," she boasts.

Wang drew her sound from English and American rock records she started listening to at thirteen, and she formed bands at school. Rock or pop had not touched China, and foreign punk was smuggled on illicit cassettes. Having been through the state-imposed Cultural Revolution and the excesses of the original Gang of Four (the ones who inspired the band from Leeds) in which anarchy did occur as students and intellectuals were banished to the rural areas, early 1990s China was emerging from twenty-five years of isolation, in which the only permitted music were folk or Cultural Revolution jingos. Inevitably, trauma and alienation ensued, accompanied by the growth of a hectic punk subculture called Yaogun, which fought to establish itself under the New China reforms known as "Socialism with Chinese

Characteristics." Control was heavy, though not always enforced. In theory, musicians could not perform without permits and were sometimes banned; any rock clubs were outlawed by definition. The Beijing punk rock scene began in the late 1980s, kickstarted by a musician called Cui Jan, whose "Nothing to My Name" (later an anthem for the Tiananmen Square protesters) helped propel Yaogun. In this edgy underground there were a few girls, but it took more than a decade for Beijing She-Punks like Wang and Hang on the Box to band together, soon to be followed by the long-running Cobra.

"Back then it was not easy for us to do music in China, and we were not welcomed either by the Chinese market. Luckily enough a Japanese record company signed and saved us," Wang says. "Otherwise I would just have had to continue my career as a designer."

Notes Jonathan Campbell, the author of *Red Rock: The Long, Strange March of Chinese Rock and Roll*, "Choosing to be in a band in 1998, whether you were male or female, was an enormous thing: society had no way of understanding/processing the idea of pursuing music in that way, and I'd argue it's quite similar even to this day. Gia was an important voice through the late '90s and into the aughts. HOTB was important for young Chinese women—and men, frankly—to see: they weren't what they were 'supposed' to be. For all the talk of the Communist idea that women hold up half the sky, they were (are, I think, still) treated appallingly."

Reprieved from her second career choice, on the speedy changes of "Asshole, I'm Not Your Baby" Wang empties her lungs in a therapeutic primal yowl, wobbly around the tuning but still forceful and melodic as she challenges. "Are you ready?" The chorus hook is primal, like 1960s surf pop. Her voice batters a wall of treated guitars that echo stomping bass. In the break, Wang plays with doubled vocals, then plunges back into the maelstrom of the title shouted/sung in English before speeding down the 4/4 rhythm freeway for the closing chorus. Throughout, she sounds gleeful, even when she stretches the slur over a surprise bluesy outro.

At her first big show in Beijing's famous Scream Club, Wang met a dashing English student and nature took its course. But when his visa was up, he had to go home for a year. Even when Wang graduated to a cell phone, in those pre-domestic internet days, communication was constant but limited. The time came for the romance to resume, to live. "I was waiting for my boyfriend in the Beijing airport, and when I saw him, I was just thinking—hey, hey, this is my BF. I think I love him, but I just don't know. What is love?" questions Wang, unconsciously echoing Gee Vaucher's anarchist response. When Wang asked herself that existential question, she threw away any pretensions of traditional good-girl-ism.

Like Crass' Vaucher, Wang questions, but via a reverse route and rationale, arriving at a diametrically opposite conclusion. Almost poignantly, Wang claims to be pro-Trump; it is doubtful he would return the favor, as the right wing he represents is generally averse to girl punks screaming abuse, no matter how cathartic it may be.

The contrarian Wang turned out to be the outsider's outsider, the only artist—not just in this book, but that I know of in the genre—to place herself squarely with the ultraconservatives. Generally, punk's free spirit does not lend itself to the authoritarianism implicit in controlling what citizens can do with their bodies. In fact, she breaks every stereotype, not just that of the submissive Asian woman but even of the She-Punk, by identifying herself as anti-abortion; one of her songs is called "Kill Your Belly." Could her position have been influenced by China's enforcement of abortion as birth control under the one-child policy from 1979 to 2015? Wang spat back, punk-style, by email, "Don't blindly imagine China unless you come to China and know China. This idea [of mine] has nothing to do with my nationality. Some people approve [of abortion] because they know nothing about the spirit and God. This so-called freedom and feminism are especially bullshit."

Well, we're all entitled to a point of view, especially in punk, even if Wang's responses were this book's most surprising, even shocking, given her artistic choices. The cooption, subversion, and degradation of the word "freedom" by its Orwellian doublethink usage on the part of repressive systems is certainly up for debate. As to "feminism"—when examined, even "Asshole, I'm Not Your Baby," Wang's crude song that shocked a nation, turns out to be rooted in the conventional morality of 1950s suburbia.

To protect herself from her soon-to-be-ex's expected negative reaction, Wang made a classic pimp move—the betrayer boomeranging their own guilt back onto the victim. Passive-Aggression 101. Still, it was all somewhat meta, Wang the "bad bitch" explains of her "good girl" rationale. "I did not mean to go out with other boys who liked me, but I did. And then I made him feel guilty. But he was not the asshole. I was."

In her case, the crude hostility turns out to be an inversion of her shame at what she somehow felt was her own "bad behavior." Yet what else is a nineteen-year-old punk girl with a boyfriend a world away supposed to do?

Having caused a sensation in the early 1990s, Wang sank from sight before reappearing to record again in the mid-2010s, like so many women here.

* * *

Unlike the intense passions displayed by Gia Wang in her unlove song, British artists tend to regard their love object with grumpy suspicion rather than hate or blissful adoration; they prod their feelings for ripeness like a melon in the market, in songs like the Gang of Four's smoocher "Love Is Like Anthrax." Famously, Boy George told the BBC that he would rather have a cup of tea than sex. Instead of the cozy UK slang term "shagging" or harsher terms for mating, the punk word for sex was "squelching"—like getting rain in your wellies from jumping in puddles, it has a playground sound.

This writer's own oft-reissued track "Launderette" captured the era's ambivalence. It depicts the sort of transient, brief encounter that seemed to mark those years for many, if not all, girl punks:

> I wanted tenpence for the dryer
> Yes, that was how we met
> My laundry bag was broken
> My clothes were soaking wet
> I felt I needed hugging
> You needed board and lodging.

The spare sound is infused with dub and the off-kilter sensation of the punky reggae I loved—the track was co-written and recorded with George Oban, the bass player of leading British reggae band Aswad. Like so many women in the book, I experienced some conflict in its making. Not because of the stellar musicians—members of the Slits, the Raincoats, Robert Wyatt, and my previous combo the Flying Lizards all honored me by playing together with my co-producers, Public Image Limited's Keith Levene and John Lydon, ex-Sex Pistol, for the first and only time. That afternoon in a Soho basement reggae recording studio was delirious fantasy fulfillment for me, marked by the exhilarating experimentation and general novelty of the event for my musical s/heroes. Oh, why did I forget my camera?

But I sang the "Launderette" vocal during "downtime" (hours when the studio is booked but not used by the artist) for the recording of Public Image Limited's 1981 album *Flowers of Romance*. For some odd reason, the engineers at Virgin Records' Manor Studios in Oxfordshire, a very elite operation, were not too happy with having to record unknown me instead of top punk Lydon, and my co-producers were still asleep. Nonetheless, I grabbed the moment and muddled through, not realizing that

my embattled first take would wind up being used on the record. But punk is a law unto itself. The song became popular
among both critics and civilians, and it was much-anthologized.
Decades on, "Launderette" was sampled by the rapper Madlib
and renamed "Filthy."

It was a relief to hear the song, many women told me, and
realize that they were not the only ones to have suddenly found
themselves almost accidentally cohabiting with a virtual stranger
for a brief, dream-like time. Then would come the disentangle-
ment process, sometimes awkward but not always, as both parties
drifted out of an experiment in intimacy. But so much of those
mid-1970s felt like—were—an experiment in living as well as
music, and all the usual courtship rituals seemed irrelevant, not
designed for the reckless times.

* * *

This invigorating climate's winds of change blew open the stage
doors for unconventional women such as the Poison Girls' Vi
Subversa, a forty-year-old mother of two when she began as a
musician. Others like Debbie Harry and Chrissie Hynde were
ready for punk, or indeed any pop moment. "I'm way past punk
and don't like being reminded of it," Hynde states. "It lasted six
months. I moved on." But if not for six months then at least
eighteen, London's punk scene fed the young American's dream
of having a band of guys of her own.

Traveling light, Hynde arrived from Akron, Ohio, via Paris
just in time for the early stirrings of punk. Before she became
famous with the Pretenders, she played in various almost-bands
with musicians including the future Sex Pistol Sid Vicious.
Bouncing around from crash pad to squat, sleeping on people's
couches (sometimes mine, as she reveals in her memoir), Hynde
was skiving on the fringes of punk, effectively homeless for peri-
ods of time. It was fantastic to hear her practice her songs in the
kitchen, and clearly, hers was a talent that would not be ignored.

Word around Hynde was that when the circumstances fit, she would be unstoppable. And so it proved to be. Her lean, androgynous good looks suited the foppish dandy '60s boy group styles she favored for a time, as well as her more usual biker/rocker approach. Her voice is creamy, knowing, and it can slap as well as stroke. She was the full package for both sub- and dom-cultures. So Hynde coincided with punk, and like the Bride of Frankenstein, it lurched towards her, arms open.

> I like the way you cross the street
> Cause you're precious
> Moving through the Cleveland heat . . .
> You're taking nights and all the kicks . . .
> But you know I was shittin' bricks
> Cause I'm precious

"Well, songs certainly mean different things to different people," says Hynde. "That's why I don't want to spoil the party by giving my meaning away." Alfred Hitchcock used to say, "Never trust the artist, trust the tale," and Hynde paints a tantalizing narrative in the three minutes of "Precious."

Chemistry sizzles as the girl and the bloke size one another up across the street. She knows that he could be a high-risk fling, but with lust heat frying her brain, she is almost ready to burn in his flame. However, there is that stab of caution as she reminds herself that the bloke's not the only precious one—she is, too: that grab at one's own self-esteem before it evaporates in steamy feelings. The split second of reserve is emphasized by Hynde's cleverness, vocal control, and range; she is on point, gliding from intimate frisson to a smoothly soaring, emotional cry on a sustained, rounded note. The band who roll with her are her first immaculately rocking gang of Pretenders, who she was rightly so proud of. The loss was unspeakable when two of them, blond guitarist James Honeyman-Scott and lanky bass player Pete Farndon, died young in drug-related circumstances. Stalwart drummer Martin Chambers continues to play with her.

Also making "Precious" special is the awareness, rare in girl punk, that sex might result in a tangible, enduring human entity—and that it might not be altogether bad. Amid the song's commanding swagger, Hynde muses, intrigued, "Maybe / I'm gonna have a baby." Potential consequences flit through the girl's mind in the second she assesses the fascinating bad boy coming towards her. The song ends on a taut freeze frame of a tantalizing drama; but the suggestion is that she will get on the back of that motorbike, or into that flatbed truck, and fling risk to the wind in the slipstream.

"How 'Precious' strengthened me was that I found I could write a song about an incident and actually benefit by something that had been rather nasty. I make a point of always getting something positive out of every experience with a man. Even if it kills me," concludes Hynde.

In a spate of punk girl memoirs by luminaries such as Sleater-Kinney's Carrie Brownstein, Sonic Youth co-founder and bass-player Kim Gordon (herself a louche, powerful den mother in the artistic circles of punk), the Slits' Viviane Albertine, and the Bags' Alicia Velasquez, there had to be a place for Chrissie Hynde, who was a rock scribe while trying to locate herself as a musician. While marketing her 2015 book *Reckless: My Life as a Pretender*, she was vilified by some feminist factions for her views on date rape.

It seemed hard for some feminists to understand that Hynde was honestly sharing her authentic experience, speaking as a woman who has directly been through a lot, looking back from a distance on her wild child years: "I've been roughed up a bit in my time, when I had no beef with the guys personally," says Hynde. "But I'd invited it, to be honest (with the aid of tons of drugs which obscured my better judgment)."

* * *

Yes, obviously all women should have the right to wear whatever they want in the street at any time. The only reason one needs to keep affirming it over and over again is because it is not reality in the early- to mid-twenty-first century, nor has it ever been thus far. Hence the vital fight for girls' agency on every level—as the following songs prove. When wearing provocative clothes it would be foolish not to be aware that one might indeed provoke a response, positive or negative. Skinny Girl Diet depict this scenario vividly in their video for "Silver Spoons." A policeman tries to feel up a PVC-clad clubber walking home alone, only to be clobbered himself by SGD's avenging angels. As such saviors are in short supply, while fighting for fairness the edgy dresser must simply always be ready for anything at all in this crazy world—or cover up coming home from the club. Either way, flat shoes are advised for quick getaways—or Doc Martens, in case you need to get kicking. As our cities get tenser, that advice is relevant for all.

Fronting her band, the Dissidents, Jakarta-born Kartika Jahja addresses the issue directly—"I wear what I want!" Liberation statements scrawled on their bodies, vibey women of all types are intercut with Jahja in her breakthrough video for 2016's "Tubuhku Otoritasku" ("My Body, My Choice"). Spontaneously, Jahja drew from the same work-with-what-you-got DIY wellspring that had moved Kathleen Hanna to perform with "Slut" on her chest in Seattle, decades before.

Many punk girls have felt impelled to write about violence against women. The whole Riot Grrrls movement began because of a home invasion and the rape of Kathleen Hanna's roommate. With men ever less sure of their place in society, violence against women only increases, as does this harsh unlove subgenre. Other examples include the yelled chorus of Bratmobile's "Shut Your Face" from 2002—"Ask if it's a girl thing / Yeah 'cos girls are dying"—and Bikini Kill's nervy "White Boy," with its Crass-like agitprop techniques of spliced 911 calls that turn the track into a drama. For Jahja, the trauma she survived inspired a song that begat several roots movements in her native Indonesia.

"Music is a big part of life in Jakarta, so you'll see guys with acoustic guitars in every street corner, just hanging out and playing music. But underline the word GUYS," Jahja stresses. "We still have a lot of negative social stigma towards women who play music. A lot of musician women in Indonesia give up their career after marriage and children."

In skewing punk, with her confrontational lyrics and semi-shaved head, Jahja is working in a local tradition. Since being turned on by a Green Day tour in the early 1990s, Indonesia has developed a tough punk underground that was spurred on by the repressive thirty-two-year regime of General Suharto that lasted until 1998. Even later, in 2011 many male and female punks, some from the large population of homeless street kids who gravitate to punk as a lifeline, were famously rounded up in the region of Acai Bandeh. Their Mohawk hair was forcibly shorn and they were sent to "reeducation camps." A year later, Jahja visited the victims with a crew from Vice UK. "A lot said they had 'converted,' but some were still punks, with their Mohawks and spikes," she recalls.

That consistency marks Jahja's progress too. She has tried various styles, but throughout any changes her punk politics remain as steady as her velvety alto, trimmed with flurries of vibrato.

"I have collaborated with some of the most respected names in the country's music industry. Played in tiny cafe gigs to football arenas. But I guess no matter what and where I sing, that punk perspective and attitude always stayed with me," Jahja says.

She and the Dissidents settled into a funky, southern R&B retro groove, flavored with a 1970s Farfisa organ sound, that frames her smooth delivery well. Though more of a jazz and soul fan as a young woman, digging Nina Simone, Jahja found herself freed by punk—she first heard the word "feminism" from Kurt Cobain—and began singing in the early 1990s.

"With punk, I felt I related so much with the sense of community. It also had a lasting political impact on me, with anarchism and the DIY ethos, some of the values I still live by to this day.

Making and trading zines, including some Riot Grrrl zines that I managed to get, really changed my perspective on a lot of things," Jahja notes. "Mind you, this was the time of the Suharto regime, when the government could make you disappear if they thought you were too radical. They confiscated leftist literature and raided discussions on campuses, but they had a blind spot for zines because they have no idea what zines are. So we were a lot more free to write radical ideas and just express whatever we wanted through these zines, which were an amazing way of cheating censorship."

The blues-rock song whose words expressed her most authentic self and drew wider attention to her, "Tubuhku Otoritasku," came about because of a repressed tragedy.

> This is my voice, my body is my authority
> What I'm shouting for is my choice
> This is for you, my best friend
> Without my permission you do not enter my territory
>
> My honor is born from my honor

"It is quite different from my previous music. For the first time, I got very explicit about what I wanted to say—no metaphors, no analogies. Yes, I experienced rape as a child, and I was silent about it until I was in my thirties," states Jahja.

> I learned from everything around me how women's bodies are often blamed for everything, from verbal harassment, to abuse, to rape—that it was my fault that I got raped. That if I spoke about it, people would not believe me. And my family would have to bear the shame of having a daughter who was raped. It doesn't help that I am also living in a culture so obsessed with virginity and female purity. So I stayed quiet. I had not realized how much that rape affected

me growing up: my sense of self-worth, my sexuality, and the way I look at life.

The repercussions caused Jahja to act out and often feel suicidal; self-medicating, she became a drug addict for much of her twenties. "We don't really have proper treatment facilities here for mental health and addiction, because it's considered to be a 'western and unreligious disease.'" Meeting Shera Rindra, a survivor who had found a way to keep achieving, galvanized Jahja. "She was no longer living in shame and self-blame the way I did," says Jahja. "That was my turning point and where my recovery began." (Rindra later became her manager.)

Masses of women poured out their experiences of abuse for the first time to Jahja after the record and newspaper article. "They had finally found a person to understand them without judgment," Jahja says. Overwhelmed, she retreated from music for two years to study gender-based violence and how to heal the trauma it causes. In 2015 she founded the Yayasan Bersama Project, a foundation to use the arts to educate the public about gender and sexuality, and collaborated with women's collectives.

Together with one such organization, Kolektif Betina, Jahja made a quick video in her bathroom, and a hashtag that went viral, drawing attention to a mass rape in a small Sumatran village that had been ignored by both government and media. As a result of the public outpouring that the women's work provoked, the government passed a new anti-sexual-violence law, with the penalty being castration. "I thought it was a stupid solution to a complex problem," observes Jahja, "done by the government just to shut down the noise."

But the attention drawn by the article and the song brought Jahja to a dangerous crossroads between being an artist and being an activist. How to balance the two proves as big a challenge as combining a private life and family with a public persona. Corporate sponsors tried to use Jahja as a shill—"the voice that cares"—and government organizations tried to "use me for their own agendas," she explains crisply. "It was a mess! That's when I learned that the kind of activism I want to do is not that which requires advocacy or policy change, or dealing with politicians. I prefer being more hands-on, being a care-giver or doing public education on gender equality, while at the same time screaming my lungs out on stage."

* * *

Schoolyard killings were born in America, yet less common are the sort of mass rapes and slaughter that Jahja fought in Indonesia; five hundred students were killed at one demonstration before Suharto finally stepped down. Still, throughout its existence the punk rock crowd, particularly in America, had become sadly habituated to ongoing individual young deaths: their own combat zone with its own mortality rate. The deeply unsettled may knowingly take their own life. Then there's that other category, dope-induced suicide by misadventure, the fate of two of Chrissie Hynde's Pretenders and twenty-four-year-old Stefanie Sargent, guitarist of Seattle's 7 Year Bitch. In 1992 singer-songwriter Mia Zapata of local band the Gits, who was something of a mentor to the younger players, wrote a song mourning Sargent. One year later, compounding the tragedy, 7 Year Bitch found themselves writing another such tribute after a friend's fatality, "M.I.A."—but this time it was to mark the murder of Zapata herself. Inner demons did not get her, but the concrete jungle did.

Finding a group, a place to fit in, is a compelling dream for outsiders and can be a heady experience when lived. Cocooned among like-minded misfits, often for the first time, it is a relief to feel that, as a group, one has helped to make a safe alternative haven beyond the regular world's judgment. But the sense of community that Seattle female punks shared turned out to be a vulnerable bubble within the city's wider problems when, as the *Seattle Times* reported, "killings are on the rise. . . . 1993 is a record year for killings."

It was with no thought of danger that Mia Zapata walked home alone late at night and was murdered after going to a club on July 7 of that year. With bold, strong features and brown eyes flashing warmth, the vivacious Zapata was an inspiration and den mother to the Seattle scene of the 1990s. Unusual for punk, her throaty, bluesy voice would have worked in an R&B band and earned her comparisons to Janis Joplin. She was clearly the real deal, and Zapata's supportiveness and sense of purpose had made her a lynchpin of a creative set that included 7 Year Bitch.

"Seattle in the late '90s was an incredibly supportive and inspiring place to be playing music or making art. There were lots and lots of bands of all kinds and many got big and famous and many more did not, but at the time no one seemed to be keeping score. There were a lot of women playing, not nearly as many as there are today, but compared to what had been happening in my local punk rock scene in the late '80s there were lots of women writing, rocking, and performing on stages and in studios," recalls Valerie Agnew, drummer of 7 Year Bitch. "There was sexism in pockets and in the industry to be sure, but despite that, there were also opportunities and new roads being forged by women every day."

The whole Seattle music community banded together to keep Zapata's case alive until forensics did jail her killer. The biggest local bands, like Pearl Jam, joined forces with the underground crowd, and an organization called Home Alive was set up to spread awareness of street violence and tactics to combat it. For several years, the operation was funded by a compilation album, *The Art of Self Defense*, released by Sony. The creative outpouring prompted by Zapata's murder included the ominous "Go Home," co-written by the Runaways' Joan Jett and Kathleen Hanna, in which a stalker is on the loose. To release their own anger and anguish, 7 Year Bitch wrote "M.I.A.": a significant artistic leap with its complex arrangements and theatricality, especially as they had very few songs, being so new. It opens with a guitar distorting as if it was wounded. With passion, singer Selene Vigil shouts the words, her voice scraped raw, hitting just out of her range and just out of tune enough with the rhythm to make a perfect harmolodic un-harmony.

> Somebody just like you gonna rape and strangle you?
> Would you mutilate yourself?
> And who would be so shocked by the brutal murder
>   of a killer?

> Will there be hundreds mourning for you?
> Will they talk of the talent and inspiration you gave?
> No. Who besides your mother will stand in sorrow
>   at your grave?

Says band bassist Elizabeth Davis of "M.I.A," "I was ready for us to stretch ourselves and do something with unusual time signatures and a different use of guitar beyond just barre chords. This was an ambitious song for us. It was also the first time I felt like the music really matched Selene's lyrics, like they were written to be put together. The lyrics are so intense and raw and the subject matter so evil. To make a song with these women about another woman who was so important to us, that reflected our feelings so cohesively and so completely, is a powerful experience."

The murder of Zapata was a loss of innocence for what had been quite an idealistic crowd. As punks, as women, attitude is natural, necessary even, to help tough out hostility; but apart from the wrenching loss, it was a shattering reminder that they were young, creative, and strong but not invulnerable, even in their cool world. The punks of Seattle were forever changed.

"Mia was tough and street smart and it was really scary to know that despite that, someone was able to do this to her," shudders Agnew.

* * *

Is a woman safe on any street late at night, anywhere? Have we ever been? Does the way we walk attract attack, and is there any "right" way to handle it? In mid-1970s America the marches began, which have now had to become global, annual events, alas. Take back the night. Reclaim the night. All prompted by street rapes and killings of women. In the early twenty-first century, *More* magazine found that only 5 percent of British women felt safe walking alone in the city after sunset. Gripping the listener as one would an attacker's throat, "The Boiler," released in 1982 by Britain's Rhoda Dakar with the Special AKA, was a chilling thematic outlier for pop. The fact that it reached number thirty-five in the British pop charts anyway shows not just the excellence of the track, but how many listeners felt its relevance. Its mass impact is all the more powerful because, as Dakar remembers, the media felt the track was as threatening as a rapist. No sooner was the song played on Saturday morning radio than, she says, "the hoo-ha started." Banned by the main radio stations for "inappropriate content," it was pulled from the shelves by the main retailers too.

"Then a story broke about it being released to coincide with a high court judge letting a guardsman off a custodial sentence for date rape, as he felt it would ruin his promising career. I was accused of cashing in," says Dakar. "I even appeared on a radio phone-in to defend my position! Of course, none of these people had any idea how long it takes for a record to be released. But that's never stopped them, before or since!"

With a bouncy sound that originated in early 1960s Jamaica, ska music is easy to love. Its distinctive on-and-off kick and gallop is a sporty beat, made all the more intriguing by the space it leaves for the jazz solos beloved by the original Skatalites at Studio One in Kingston, who created it. Two decades later in Britain, the home of Jamaica's old colonial ruler, the updated ska made by multiracial groups collectively known as 2 Tone became a route to an instant audience, with bands like Madness, the Specials, and Selecter embracing the style. Singer Dakar, who wrote "The Boiler" with her girl ska band the Bodysnatchers, was not raised with the music. But it became a passport for the young drama student; an already spot-lit stage on which she could perform an identity of borrowed "blackness."

"I was a big pop fan at secondary school. Apart from the obligatory 'Natty Dread' by Bob Marley and the Wailers (the Jamaican band's second international LP), I was more into David Bowie, Alice Cooper, New York Dolls, Lou Reed." Dakar explains.

I had heard Jamaican music in the local streets from the record shops and, as we lived nearby, from the Ram Jam Club when the windows were open. At primary school in '69/'70, we danced to early reggae in the playground by singing the hits of the day. A couple of the cool boys wore Ben Sherman shirts, Levi's, braces, and monkey boots [the ska-loving skinhead style]. Apart from Millie's "My Boy Lollipop," which my cousin Janice took me to buy at the Brixton record shop Desmond's Hip City—she'd seen Millie live in Lagos, Nigeria—to me, ska was "old people music." I'm still not a great fan.

As they split up after one year and two singles, the Bodysnatchers could be dismissed as a novelty flash-in-the-pan riding on the ska fad's coattails; except the band had real talent, and for Dakar it proved a genuine launchpad. She went on to sing with the Specials and continues to perform and release music independently—after the sort of time gap so common in this book.

"I think starting off my career in an all-female environment normalized it for me. The band that made me think I could be in one too was the Mo-Dettes, as I knew Kate and June already and had heard they were looking for a singer. I didn't quite have the front to put myself forward. Women inspire women. Sometimes you end up having to be a sort of geezer bird to get by. I don't have to any more, as I'm in charge," says Dakar.

"The Boiler" was the Bodysnatchers' first song, and the only original they played in their first show. But at the time she finally recorded it, Dakar had come off the road singing with the 2 Tone movement's founders, the Specials, and was testing out a solo career before joining its main man Jerry Dammers's next project. The sound is Specials-era ska, meaning its horn section's sensibility was drenched in arrangements like John Barry's 1960s James Bond theme tunes. Not based on any particular true story, but painfully real for all that, the song is uneasy listening. Part of its power stems from the tension between its sound, ska, usually associated with good cheer, and its grim subject matter, date rape. The scariest aspect of one of the most dramatic songs ever recorded is not only the rape in itself, or even the tension building up to it, but the unnamed protagonist's own subbasement self-love. When the bloke starts to manhandle the girl, she rejects him. He counters with the classic blame-the-victim pimp move that Gia Wang used on "Asshole, I'm Not Your Baby": he sneers at her and walks off. It worked this time, too:

"Come back to my place, I only live just 'round
the corner
You can go home in the morning, yeah?"
"Well I don't think so, I mean I've only known you a day,
It's a bit soon innit? . . ."
But then he starts to get mad
"Listen here girl, I bought that gear you got on,
I paid you in here tonight . . ."

Opening in a relaxed conversational style, Dakar builds up suspense as the simple human drama unfolds and seems like it could be leading up to a Prince Charming finale. The reality is . . . well, hear and fear for yourself. Dakar was experienced in working a theatrical audience. "Before being in a band, I had been part of the Old Vic Youth Theatre and had experience of improvisation. 'The Boiler' was an improvisation set to music. I had never written songs with a band, so it was an intermediary effort between theatre, which I knew as a participant, and music, which I knew as a spectator. As time went on, the improvisation became solidified, to the extent I could perform it live on TV to a pre-recorded backing track," she says.

While Tika Jahja and Kathleen Hanna found that their music about violence against women triggered a flood of previously concealed confessions, Dakar's musical catharsis prompted a rather different response. "I don't remember any women talking to me about their experiences. My audiences were mostly male and when they heard 'The Boiler'; they were usually a bit shell shocked."

* * *

The sequential styles that have sprung from the musical powerhouse of Jamaica, such as ska, reggae, and dub, gave a language to Rhoda Dakar that she experiments with in "The Boiler." The reverberations of Jamaica's creativity are disproportionate to its size. Something innate in its identity has made its cultural impact greater than that of any other Caribbean island with the exception of Cuba.

The island's revolutionary Rasta movement also charged the energy of Alicia Velasquez, a.k.a Alice Bag, a theatrically inclined young Chicana punk in comparatively distant Los Angeles. As Bag uses Rasta spirituality to taunt those she's addressing on "Babylonian Gorgon"—it could be one individual, a lover even, or society—she mixes mythic metaphors to evoke the menace of

Babylon, the evil, rapacious system of Rasta cosmology (you can call it neoliberalism in the early twenty-first century). Although the Jamaican community in Los Angeles back then was comparatively small, Rasta mystique percolated through from the UK and the pages of the LA punk magazine *Slash*, co-founded by a collective including a reggae-obsessed Frenchman Claude Bessy and his wife, Philomena Winstanley.

An ambiguity trembles through "Babylonian Gorgon"; Bag seems to address both a potentially threatening individual who somehow *feels* male—a lover?—and the patriarchy at once. If it is a potential relationship, the suspicious Bag is putting her suitor through rigorous tests. Is it a rapist or a trigger-happy nosy neighbor? Rage and terror throb beneath the track's pumping muscle like a vein about to explode.

> Don't want your private lives.
> Don't want your industrial lies.
> Your politician dreams,
> Your psychodrama schemes.
> One false move, you're gonna die!
> Here I go, Babylonian gorgon. I'm gonna babble babble on.

Of the various first-wave punk scenes, Los Angeles was the most theatrical, with its trash aesthetic born of Frederick's of Hollywood, at that stage America's main racy lingerie store. Hot punk news would pogo first between London and New York, and then hop across the continent to finally land in Hollywood. South of Los Angeles, around Orange County, a very macho hardcore had come to be synonymous with punk—the sort of rugby scrum testosterone mosh pit that prompted the Riot Grrrl call "Girls to the front!" The Hollywood scene was seemingly semi-invented by two chatty, clever, yet still somewhat sinister, arbiters: veteran producer/songwriter Kim Fowley, who assembled the Runaways, and radio DJ Rodney Bingenheimer, whose Rodney's English Disco became punk central to the local music-loving waifs and strays. Due to the predatory tastes of the two far older men, much of the LA scene seemed to revolve around near-underage girls in the sort of lingerie rocked in public by both the Go-Go's and the Runaways: a far cry from the rugged revolutionist spirit of British girl punks and the monochrome opacity favored by New Yorkers. In its vast sprawl, as writer Evelyn McDonnell notes in her *Queens of Noise* book about the Runaways, simply putting a band together meant being very committed; it was logistically daunting, especially for a low- to no-income teen without a car. The Runaways' frothy punk-rock fun had its own giggly energy, and they became among the most commercial She-Punks. To some outsiders, with their Lolita frisson, both bands' punk credentials rang slightly phony—as if they had been assembled like nubile Stepford Punkettes, not so much to mock the cheesy fantasies of Fowley and his cronies, but to pander to them with tracks like "Cherry Bomb." Undoubtedly gifted and charismatic, his demons were whispered of but only fully exposed in the year of his death, 2015. While partiers including bandmate Joan Jett looked on, Fowley had raped her, stated Jackie Fuchs (a.k.a. Fox) in a *Huffington Post* interview—a claim Jett denied but others confirmed. Amid the murky swirl of LA's rococo decadence, with Hollywood glitz overlaying the glitter, maybe the hard facts will always remain blurry. But somehow the sleaze, the abuse, was no surprise.

Though they grew up with Bingenheimer, LA kids Belinda Carlisle and the Go-Go's ultimately signed with a female manager, Ginger Canzoneri; strong-minded LA punks like X's Exene Cervenka and the Cramps' Poison Ivy avoided the pedophilic Fowley concept that was often seen as central to LA's trash aesthetic. Almost lured into Fowler and Bingenheimer's Svengali clutches, Alice of the Bags stayed the music course to mature into a performer, author, and activist. The band name came because they first performed with grocery bags over their heads as a (Situationist?) prank. The humble, utilitarian brown paper seemed a symbolic representation of how Chicano women artists were essential but ignored, neglected, even negated by the dominant system. A band like Bag's meant resistance in fishnets.

For those used to feeling like outsiders, glam, then punk, provided a release, a direction that would ultimately empower Bag—virtually the only Chicana punk of her generation—decades on to produce a second generation of Chicana girl punks, the group Fea, with Joan Jett for her Blackheart label.

Like so many others, Bag lost roommates and friends of both sexes to over-partying, often from drug overdoses whose murky motivation would always haunt their coterie. One such loss was fellow scene originator, the Germs' singer Darby Crash. Somehow, the Los Angeles punk scene often seemed the most hedonistic and decadent of all.

"Fun was a big part of it, for sure! I can't speak for everyone, but I was young and stupid when I first got into punk. My field of view was much more narrow then; I didn't know much about my place in the world or how my government's actions affected other countries," Bag reflects. "I was coming from glam, which had all the political sensitivity of the French court before the revolution. Punk in LA wasn't intentionally political at first, though the fact that it had a lot of diversity made it socially relevant. I think the scene did grow to be more political, especially as the 1980s rolled around and a certain right-wing actor became commander in chief."

In one song, she writes "We Don't Need the English," a punk response to the cultural domination that had by now switched somewhat from New York to London, whose bands were worshipped on their visitations to the distant West Coast. Nonetheless, the received wisdom of Britain formed Bag, arguably as much as her Mexican heritage.

"Watching David Bowie helped me appreciate the sensuous side of androgyny. He was also the first person to talk about bisexuality, which was a term I had never heard of before. I felt validated. I was a teen at the time, experiencing pangs of sexual attraction that went beyond the acceptable heterosexual limits, so to hear Bowie speak of bisexuality as something that was normal and healthy was especially important," reflects Bag. "Where glam was about skill, show production, and general excess, punk stripped things down to their essentials. Rebellion, creativity, rawness—these were the essentials of punk. Punk allowed me to see that the only limitations were ones that I placed on myself."

The magical mystery of glam helped Alicia Velasquez transition from the irregular yet traumatic ghetto roughness around her, but ultimately punk was the channel for her liberation. Like hookers on Hollywood Boulevard in 1940s films, Alice Bag sported corsets, garter belts, and fishnets onstage—but somehow, probably because she seemed like a grown woman, unlike the Runaways, Bag owned them differently; the boudoir wear looked consciously provocative, not like she was conforming to some much older man's idea of what's hot. And as she became more sophisticated, she also engaged with a wider world.

"My bands were frequently asked to play fundraisers to benefit social and political organizations. Those benefit concerts raised consciousness as well as funds. I remember doing several concerts for an organization called CISPES (Committee in Solidarity with the People of El Salvador). CISPES provided aid to the people of El Salvador who were fighting against a corrupt government which was being kept in place by the Reagan administration."

A key song on Alice Bag's first and only original album is "Violence Girl," after which she named her memoir. In time, she made her peace with her loving, nonetheless toxic, home environment. Her father's frustration and taste for alcohol encouraged his abuse of her mother, who would never leave, however Bag begged. In their final years, as her father weakened, their marriage grew stronger: a codependent by-product of the sort of social structure and relationships that Bag whips on "Babylonian Gorgon."

Her delivery is knowing, dramatic; she enunciates with a growl—the lion who tames. And yet, for "Babylonian Gorgon," the East LA Catholic girl borrowed foreign Rasta imagery. The concept of Babylon, the corrupt capitalist patriarchy, was familiar not only because of the West Coast's growing West Indian community, or even due to the influence of *Slash* magazine, but also because of the absorption into the musical bloodstream of white UK punk bands such as the Slits and the Raincoats. And because the revelatory, apocalyptic imagery and energy of the Rastas spoke to Bag too. Yet one native Jamaican, Grace Jones, had to leave the island and return, to best enjoy its allure.

* * *

Presenting themselves as commanding dominatrixes in control of their destiny, both Grace Jones and Alice Bag cracked whips onstage. But both women's power was hard won. In Jamaica and in Los Angeles, both Jones and Bag had to overcome the sting of harsh punishment in their childhood, whether it was mental— Bag having to protect her mother—or a literal whip in Jones's case. When Jones's parents moved to America, they left her in Jamaica to be raised in the countryside by her strict Christian grandparents. Jones' grandfather was of the old school. He believed in tough discipline as preparation for the cruelty of life; the set of whips on his wall had one to fit each child in his care.

Onstage, Jones might choose to use them, but she needs no props to dominate an audience. It takes only her contemptuous gaze and imperious pose. Her compelling persona aside, Jones is also hilariously funny.

"Returning to Jamaica does bring certain things back," she recalled as we sat one sultry Jamaican night by the beach at Chris Blackwell's Oracabessa hotel, Goldeneye. "Don't forget when I grew up, people were afraid of Rastas. I was told to run and hide under the bed when dreads came by on their bicycles—like a Hell's Angels gang on Harley Davidsons! I had different comparisons after I had been out and in the world. I did the Harley Davidson thing! What is so frightening? They didn't look as frightening as the Rastas, and they were on bicycles," she laughed. "Can you imagine if they were on Harleys?"

Wit was always a weapon in Jones' arsenal. But despite appearances, Jones wasn't tough all of the time. One of the most charismatic and formidable *femmes* on the planet sobbed against the elevator wall in a converted factory on Manhattan's Union Square as I interviewed her for *Harpers & Queen* magazine in 1982. It was an odd disconnect between the image, the music, and the woman. Not an hour before, the model and disco queen bringing a new dimension to pop had volunteered to crawl along the building's penthouse parapet, many stories above the busy city, snarling for the camera. The downtown Manhattan loft aerie belonged to a Frenchman, Jean-Paul Goude, soon to be her husband. He was her Svengali, a designer and visionary whose startling imagery of his muse helped confirm her stardom.

Jones and Goude would always remain close; their son, Paolo, grew up to perform with her, and she glows as she describes writing songs with him. But like most couples, let alone those who work together, there were stormy moments, and this was one. "He always wants me to be an animal!" she cried in the elevator. Sometimes the Amazonian Jones just wanted to be soft and womanly, and apparently, back then Goude did not know how to handle this shift in the indomitable diva whom he adored, who would soon be called on to embody woman warriors in epic action movies.

Goude saw in her the perfect blend of yin and yang, and his divinely simple stylings—Jones with a flat-top haircut, looking like a boxer, a cigarette drooping from her mouth; Jones with a glass of champagne balanced on her bum, emphasizing its orb (a pose he later dared to try and replicate with Kim Kardashian). Together, they reimagined Jones as an icon for everyone, whose highly stylized, transgressive Afro-futurist force field spread beyond gender and color while burrowing deeply into both. But for a moment in that elevator, Jones was teetering over what suddenly seemed a chasm, experiencing femme feelings when her man was expecting a bit more butch. Jones would find a way to resolve that tension, just by continuing to be her inimitable self, a rare free spirit for whom what seems "performance" to outsiders is actually reality.

When Jones began singing in the mid-1970s, she cut ravishing disco hits like "La Vie en Rose" at the fabled Sigma Sound Studios, home of the Sound of Philadelphia, with masters of the string section Gamble and Huff. Working with masters of the game, she saw herself as a cog in the music machine and was insecure about her voice. A Jamaican, Jones was also cautious about returning long-term to the site of many painful associations. The autonomy she had always craved only came to her once she left the island. But her label boss, Chris Blackwell of Island Records (whom she introduced to his wife, Mary) had been instrumental in releasing the reggae that transformed punks' lives and art, and now he was able to stir the same pot in the opposite direction: helping return Jones to her roots as a "big 'ooman" (full-grown woman).

Discovering Jamaica anew was exhilarating for Jones without her family's heavy church constraints. In her memoir, she denies rumors swirling about her love affairs—but there is more than one way to be intimate, and Harry doesn't always have to shag Sally at the end. When I was on the island at the time, Jones looked happy, renewed even, hanging out with "her Jamaican guy"—in whatever capacity.

> Take a toke from the smoke,
> Never standing by the door,
> Just stretching out pan de floor,
> That way him don't fall over,
> No way him gwan fall out pan me . . .
> My Jamaican guy, My Jamaican guy.

Jones explains,

> "My Jamaican Guy" was inspired by a moment while I was in the Bahamas, recording at Chris Blackwell's Compass

Point Studios. I was at his house, sitting in a lounge chair by his swimming pool, and the Wailers' keyboard player, Tyrone Downie, came out from under the water, and he shook his dreads—like when a dog comes out of water and does that shaking thing?

It was one of the most beautiful sights that I ever saw; it seemed in slow motion to me, visually. That is when I wrote "My Jamaican Guy" in my head. Tyrone wasn't mine, but he was mine by association with Jamaica. Then after having that one line, it was OK, where do I go from here? Because I didn't have a girlfriend/boyfriend relationship, it was basically a visual affair I had with Tyrone at that moment, coming out of the water. Later on, I did fall in love with a Jamaican guy [with satisfaction]. It's like I predicted him.

The second verse was inspired by a party at Compass Point, at which Jones noted that the smokers would recline to enjoy their spliffs. With relish, Jones quotes her song, "'Laid back, not thinking back . . . laid back but never holding back . . .' Of course, the music brings the words in by itself. You can hear the music in the wind with these words. It was one of the first songs where I wrote the music and lyrics. I have to give credit to the musicians who watched me come into the studio with just a little piece of paper."

The bass on "My Jamaican Guy" sucks at you like quicksand, with a fat, wobbly gulp; the crisp drums keep you guessing, grabbing fresh rhythms from bar to bar. The unmistakable sound was made by the Compass Point All-Stars, on this occasion being guitarist Barry Reynolds and imaginative French-African synthesizer whiz Wally Badarou, on whose haunting intro motif the song was based. Their foundation was bassist Robbie Shakespeare and drummer Sly Dunbar, known as the Riddim Twins, playing with digital drums programmed to sound like cicadas—literally. It was a fusion world, where Lizzy Mercier Descloux would also soon flourish. In the blandness of genteel Nassau, tropical funk could develop amid palm trees and piña coladas, without the ever-present stress of, say, downtown Kingston's recording studios.

Usually as unsure of her writing as she was of her singing, Jones blossomed on "My Jamaican Guy." The lyrics are simple, but to achieve their effect, the brief verses strung between the repetitions of "My Jamaican Guy" are sufficient. Jones repeats the title, deadpan yet smoldering, over that commanding rhythm. Top reggae rhythm section Dunbar and Shakespeare give the tune an incantatory power, summon the urgent heat beyond words between two people realizing how they complement each other. In its comfort with the groove and sheer relaxation, like muttering meaningless baby talk to a beloved, it suggests a special intimacy—and Jones finally being at ease with her roots and her romance. As she lists his attributes, one senses that, flipping traditional gender roles, Jones has picked this *bred'ren* as her consort, for as long as he stays "laid back."

* * *

In first-wave UK punk, though couples were known to form—Nancy Spungen and Sid Vicious being a sad, bad example—it was fashionable to regard sex as something quite normal between pals, to be gossiped about, sure, but not judged moralistically. In fact, that would be unpunk, as freedom was part of the package. Sex, punk style, suggests a quick, messy encounter—having it off in club toilets or grotty squats, as most punks did not have deluxe accommodation. And so it went on till the early 1980s, when AIDS slapped some of that fun in the face, along with Thatcher, Reagan, and the neoconservatism that was to plunge the world into often baseless wars that would ravage much of Africa and the Middle East. Its repercussions were to horrify the early twenty-first century world and change the face of Europe.

If all the old courtship rules seemed to be suspended in the 1970s, freed by penicillin and the pill and the not-yet existence of AIDS, the loss of innocence brought about by twenty-first-century internet porn and the prevalence of easy come, easy go "squelching" partners on dating sites made flowers-and-chocolate romancing seem as long gone as the crinoline. The developments of the next century would open uncharted territories for both love and unlove, negotiating new patterns of being and relating that had been literally impossible in the previous century. Even when punk began, the medically enhanced gender fluidity available to bands like San Francisco's Tribe 8 in the early twenty-first century was deeply exotic, only known to be obtainable in Brazil at vast expense. At the end of punk's birth century, adventurers would romp on its wild gender frontier.

Punk haunts across England in the 1970s were often gay clubs, like the Sombrero on Kensington High Street or Club Louise in London's Soho. The subculture was now legal, and the gay rights movement was gathering force; but homosexuality still lurked slightly in the shadows as attitudes were slow to catch up with legislation, and gay-bashing was as popular among violent skinheads as "Paki-bashing" (scarily casual slang for beating up South Asians).

Despite the legalization of homosexuality in 1967, writer and punk aficionado Jon Savage recalls, "Punk was no particular help in Britain's hostile climate. Despite the fact that many early participants were gay or bisexual, British punk was not sympathetic to homosexuality. The time was super exciting, but what I remember most, forty years on, is punk's conspiracy of silence. Nobody seemed to talk about homosexuality. Feminism yes, but not gay rights or gay consciousness. Punk songs on gay topics were all coded and somehow marginal."

So no gay genre arose in the first UK punk wave. But all that would change. The early twenty-first century is an intriguing time to be considering love in punk music, or love at all. Ancient Greek, Japanese Kabuki, and British Shakespeare's female dramatic roles were traditionally played by boys. But the transgender men giving birth and feeding their babies, who are rare but not unknown in the early twenty-first century, would have seemed the stuff of futurist writers like Octavia E. Butler or Margaret Atwood to those gender-slipping forebears.

Gender-fluid artists flourished then in the silver-lined womb of Warhol's New York Factory, an avant-garde art conveyor belt with a queer sensibility: glamorous transgender actress Candy Darling, who died in 1974; Jayne, who became Wayne County, a CBGB regular who transplanted her glam self to London in 1977, punk's zenith, and formed the band the Electric Chairs. County's peroxide presence enabled the glam New York Dolls, basically straight dudes who dug drag, to sport suspenders just before punk.

Oh no—not more competition! The cry goes up among males alarmed by having to work twice as hard to attract a woman. No wonder the less secure section of the straight male population fear the arrival of the many-gender planet. Theorists will insist that this multiplicity of sexual personae were always there, just suppressed, and that may be so. But the early twenty-first century represents a pan-gender flowering, in which gender is key to artists' personae. The many-gender cat is out of the binary bag and is roaming the globe. After over ten years of fronting her rock band, Against Me!, as a self-identified man, the bold public transition of Gainesville, Florida's Laura Jane Grace in 2012 was a landmark because the fans followed her so faithfully. Her musical style was the same, and the rocker took her audience along for the ride to understanding gender ambiguity. Grace's clarity was a pivotal factor in an increased awareness of the porous boundaries between genders separated by chromosomes, social conditioning, or whatever it takes. It also raises the question of what, if anything, makes music specifically female. It remains to be heard if the sound of future recordings will reflect Grace's physical change.

Climaxing the rambunctious "Check Out Your Babe," a 1992 track by San Francisco's Tribe 8, is a raucous playlet about dueling member size between male and maybe female. Now choosing to be known by the pronouns *they* or *he*, singer-songwriter Lynne

Breedlove delivered "Your Girlfriend's Hot" as a butch woman. Breedlove's confrontational sneer and snarl locate the song in the alley at the back of a club. They're ready for a rumble. With authority, they stride through musical changes, switching gears from a chunky, guitar-propelled mid-tempo, zooming up to a punk frenzy as the lyrics depict not simply a spurious rivalry, but an analysis of the ways in which the bloke is belittling the girl. Ultimately, it transpires that the battle is about basic caring and respect.

In the vivid narrative of "Your Girlfriend's Hot" straight guys had better lock up their girlfriends, as the hot dykes were in the club, on a mission to convert. "That was kind of a legend in our own mind, I guess," modestly confesses their guitarist, Silas Howard. "But we watched a new scene evolving, certainly in the cities, with bands like L7 and Bikini Kill." Soon, Tribe 8 themselves would become key to another new gender expression scene, queer- or homo-core.

The witty drama of Tribe 8 songs extended to their onstage theatricality. They tried to turn every venue into some approximation of a rowdy S&M dyke bar. The documentary *Rise Up* documents their gender-spoofing antics: mock castrations and persuasion of a heterosexual male audience member to fellate a dildo. Given their vivid satire of male stereotypes, it may be surprising to some that Flipper, the band's guitarist, chose to transition into one of the much-teased species, but living his own masculinity as a transman was a long-cherished dream. Becoming Silas Howard, the guitarist moved into directing TV, movies, and documentaries, often on transgender themes.

"I jokingly call myself a fake male, though it is not politically correct," laughs Howard. "I don't identify as either straight or male in that [patriarchal] way." Jokes are key to Tribe 8. Even the title of the album on which the song appears, *Snarky*, shows they wanted to present arguably marginal ideas with a spoonful of humor to make them go down.

Recalls Howard, "Being really goofy was an important part of our personality, just being sarcastic. Not taking things seriously.

We had a love of paradox—that's what allowed us to record tracks like 'Your Girlfriend's Hot' and [the more stridently political] 'Lezbophobia.' We were playing lots of straight spaces which embraced us. We were always outsiders, to gay people, to straight people—we were a new phenomenon. Humor allowed people to be part of it, our passport." Howard continues,

> Because we didn't fit in anywhere, we got to go everywhere, creating this new space between queer and punk. Straight people who didn't understand our humor—even we didn't, sometimes!—still got the energy and the attitude. After a while, it became cool to be queer.
>
> I am a masculine presentation now, but I appreciate masculinity, femininity, androgyny, all those expressions. I was never successful as a female, until I found my queer butch punk identity. I feel both genders, the whole way. I'm not going to deny my history. I love the idea of Women in Punk; if someone wants to involve me, hey, I am always glad. If anything, transitioning has made me more avidly feminist.

Making their mark at the time of third-wave feminism in the 1990s, Tribe 8 were witty warriors in the vanguard of a rapidly evolving society. "Diversity gets commodified and people get discounted," Howard says. "But in Tribe 8, we were queer and trans, all together. So few in numbers, but we saved each other's asses. That is just my pack," he concludes, in a fine display of humanhood.

* * *

Using humor and confrontation, Tribe 8 negotiated 1990s boundaries on the new gender frontier. But even the old binary gender frontier often needed a map. The feisty 1970s, with its attitudinal punk stance, would give way to the more polished

1980s, with its more slippery, "me-terialism" values. Towards the very end of the rough 'n' tough first punk time, on the cusp of the self-centric new decade of Reagan/Bush and Thatcher, two short-lived but long-loved girl (or equal-gendered) bands showed how different punk women's views can be.

The leftist axis in Britain's early 1980s post-punk world produced the bracing, egalitarian love songs one would hope for from a community where men were expected to at least act liberated. Those years saw creative positives like the rise of hip-hop and a growing awareness of non-Anglophone "world" music. However, as the decade progressed, there also came the rollback of women's progress (including the near-neutralization of the original wild girls of punk), which writer Susan Faludi described in 1991 in her bestselling book *Backlash*. Her fellow feminist thinker, Naomi Wolf, put it thus in a *New York Times Magazine* article, "The Future Is Ours to Lose": "The predictable backlash came, as it always does; the evil 80s were a time of shoulder pads, silicone and retrenchment. Again—so quickly, so thoroughly— women 'forgot.'"

Lesley Woods and the Au Pairs lived it. "There really was a backlash against the preceding era, when it had started to become quite left wing and progressive. That's normally what happens. Thatcher's children came along, the yuppies. You had to be successful, corporate, with a nice house and a nice car. It went back to those pretentious values, run by the ones we had been shouting at and saying they were bollocks," states Woods.

The forceful brunette singer-songwriter made socially conscious pop for a decade and then entered a politically charged profession as an immigration lawyer in London. "I started in 1992 and I have never known it to be so draconian as in the mid-2010s." Woods has noted our cultural climate's progress.

When the Au Pairs began, we didn't have any of these "isms"—age, sex, and sexuality discrimination. It's completely swung around. I'm just saying it is a very simple fact. People were not legally protected the way they are now. Abortion and homosexuality had recently been legalized, but when one was writing these songs, wives could still be raped by their husbands. Women could not buy property unless their father or husband signed for them. To me, many of these gender issues are so improved that if I was a young woman now in a band like the Au Pairs, surrounded by other creators, and we all shared the same values and anger, I would be singing about other struggles, like immigration. Child sex trafficking. Equal pay for women. But we had a lot to be angry about.

"We were all very angry, partly because we came from the generation whose parents had engaged in the Second World War and the Holocaust," she continues. "How could they have let that happen? How could they not support human rights and the struggle? I did not see my mum and dad going on demos."

Yes, even a conservative would have to admit that being a female punk musician is easier within leftist circles, in which equality is the default mode (whether people betray those ideals or not). That healthier reality shines out of "It's Obvious," the Au Pairs keynote track on their 1981 album, hailed as exemplifying the state of progressive pop's art, *Playing with a Different Sex.* Writers Simon Reynolds and Joy Press call it "agit-funk." Like the bands to whom they were often compared, Leeds leftists the Gang of Four and their "sister" group the Delta 5, the music of the Au Pairs was very sparse, with melody lines that jump unexpectedly and crisp lyrics. Grounded in a remorseless yet tuneful bass line counterpointed by nervy guitar, the Au Pairs mix is spiked with free jazz saxophone. The drumming is understated, played mostly on the top of the kit. It seems like it could just be a fragile web of sound held together with duct tape, but it is strong as any rock.

Spending time nowadays, by myself
That's oh so nice

And again with you, it's equal nice
It's paradise . . .
You're equal but different
It's obvious, it's obvious

In the song, Woods paints an affirmative, if ironic, vision of the world as they want to see it, and as it sometimes appeared to be in their immediate, equality-conscious circles. "It's a positive song and it covers all sort of situations," she points out. As well as being about love, it also "summed up our feelings about what was going on at the time: rights of women, blacks, gays, apartheid, Northern Ireland, the miners' strike, squatters. There was a lot of conflict."

"My feeling was, we were all on the same side," she says of the Delta 5, Gang of Four, the Mekons, and the Bush Tetras in New York. However, the wider world could be more hostile.

I grew up in a generation where boys would sit in the back of cars with you and try to get your knickers down. Often they were the sort of boys who would play on a bill with us when we started out, and they could not cope with women in bands. They would be very dismissive, then when you showed you weren't going to sing nice and pretty, that you were angry and representing assertively, they didn't like that either. They were very threatened by it.

But we worked with fantastic men, and I had wonderful boyfriends and lovers. When the liberation movements took off in the 1960s, women's role was to fuck the guys the night before they went off to plant a bomb. By the time the guys who were political like the Gang of Four came along in the 1980s, they realized they had to embrace women's politics and sexual politics too.

The band formed in 1977 when Woods met guitarist Paul Foad at a bus stop. They soon found complementary musical skills and ideas, and mutual passion as well. Once forming a band was obvious, they committed to being split-gender and had to search for "the only female bass player in Birmingham," who turned out to be Jane Monroe.

"I had just got into left-wing feminism as a really young woman, probably very unworldly. I was reading a lot of Marge Piercy and Simone de Beauvoir, and thinking, 'Wow, this is great,'" Woods explains. The Au Pairs became respected stalwarts of Rock Against Racism and other causes. Notes Woods, "We weren't going 'round apologizing like a lot of bands. Some people thought politics was boring and bands who sang about it were boring, ramming things down your throat. The Au Pairs were political and not ashamed of it."

∗ ∗ ∗

"Some people" would be the Mo-Dettes, who were determined to keep punk more girly-girly and reclaim the romping, carousing giggles that Cyndi Lauper would soon herald in her 1983 track "Girls Just Wanna Have Fun," a demo of which by its writer, Robert Hazard, was cut in 1979, the same year as the Mo-Dettes' "White Mice." As the name suggests, their style and imagery fit into regular femininity, hovering between soft pastels and *yé-yé*, as the French called their naturally chicer version of Britain's swinging '60s/mod aesthetic.

Mo-Dettes' guitar player Kate Korris is an ex-member of both the Raincoats and the Slits. Using the funk phrase to mean self-righteous political correctness, she scoffs,

> "'Right on' so often comes off as miserable, reactive, and condescending. As if only rebellious females could count for anything!" . . . It was a feminist who dissed us as "bored housewives." Men could be much more accepting allies. After the Slits, I moved away from the all-girl idea. It seemed to place us in a kind of "freak" status that felt

unnatural to me. But in trying out players to form a band with the drummer June Miles-Kingston, we couldn't find guys who weren't either scared or trying to dominate us. We weren't all girls because of a premeditated stance, but because we found no suitable males available. The bass player, Jane Perry Crockford [later Woodgate], was having a similar experience, and we gravitated toward each other.

Their "meet cute" typified the times. Recalls Woodgate, chuckling, "We bumped into each other in the dole queue at Lisson Grove. Kate already had a drummer—June—and I had a singer, Ramona Carlier. We first played together in the Sex Pistols' rehearsal room, right in the heart of London's music scene, Tin Pan Alley."

The young women were embedded in the heart of the first punk insurgency. The Clash's singer-songwriter Joe Strummer showed the novice Korris a couple of guitar chords, and advised, "You can do anything with those two pieces of info; go for it." "And he was right!" laughs Korris. "Fighting for 'equality' actually defines you as seeing yourself as 'less than.' Joe imparted empowerment, not supervision. Back then, as far as other artists were concerned, the field felt level and inclusive. Fans likewise. Our basic 'agenda' was that we were individuals making music. We didn't identify with punk, feminism, or any particular genre. Hell, we barely identified with each other!" Subscribing to neither bourgeois individualism nor left-wing collectivism, then, the Mo-Dettes felt they functioned outside the system and cared not for the majority's opinion, even that of their peers. Their pretty punkitude was more existential, grounded in their individual experiences and analyses.

"If there was a message to/about girls, it was that being female is not something to apologize for or cover up. You don't have to be butch or loony to stand up for your female self. You can still like boys, wear skirts and makeup, and be your own person.

'Playing like a girl' is just as good as playing 'like a man,'" Korris concludes.

The Mo-Dettes loved to subvert leftist orthodoxies.

"My life was about picking up and seducing boys, and I thought, let's turn it 'round! Our label's distributors, Rough Trade, were very enthusiastic about us—but even there, some of the feminist workers disapproved, saying we were sexist," recalls a still-amazed Woodgate. A particular cis-girly sexual assertiveness subverts the Mo-Dettes' cheery singalong girl group harmonies and ringing surf guitars. "I was a horny twenty-two-year-old girl sitting in the pub and thinking about picking up boys. I was so fed up with boys being the dominant ones to pull women," says Woodgate indignantly. "I can be very predatory myself, seeing a cute young boy and saying, 'Hey, wanna play with me?' I avoided feminism *because* I believe a woman's essence is as strong as any man's. Really, I have been a feminist all my life—I believe in equal pay and rights—but at the time I couldn't identify with the movement because there were too many labels and disapproving factions." Post Mo-Dettes, Woodgate became a mature art school student, gained an MA, and later worked with organic food; obviously, her performance of "predatory" is different from Harvey Weinstein's.

Before co-founding the Mo-Dettes, Korris had already passed through the ranks of not only the Slits and the Raincoats, but also the Derelicts, who later split into PragVEC and the Passions, known for their hit sung by Barbara Gogan, "I'm in Love with a German Film Star." Experience helped shape the cheeky sass of "White Mice." The song demonstrates that like Grace Jones, these girls prefer to pick their partners.

Now it's said, it's straight to bed
No need to make it harder . . .
Don't be stupid, don't be limp
No girl likes to love a wimp

Dance and make fun, nicely done
Come and be my number one

"White Mice" struts and bounces on a rolling bass, doubled by Korris's twangy guitar, which suggests the open chords of surf pop. Replete with faux-nostalgic backing vocals *à la* '60s girl groups, Woodgate's lyrics exude the entitlement of the young and the beautiful—or the confident, anyway. At the dance, instead of waiting eagerly to be asked by the bloke, this girl's attitude is "Show us what you got." She knows what she wants and is not afraid to ask. It is sung with a naughty challenge that feels very modern.

"The melody was mine, written in counterpoint to Jane's bass line, which was the framework of the song," recalls Korris. "Afterwards, the Flying Lizards' David Cunningham put the guitar through a phaser; supposedly this was to even up the rhythm. One of my ongoing battles was with folk who preferred 'steady' to spontaneous rhythm. But on this track, I liked the result. Otherwise, the track was cut straight."

And that's where "straight" ended, as the band soon lost their way with misguided management and insensitive record companies.

Says Korris, "The auxiliary professionals around us seemed to think we needed molding. Many of them didn't seem to realize we weren't trying to sound like their idea of rock 'n' roll. I think they actually considered themselves to be supportive." Among the conflicts was the label's idea that the band should put themselves up for the middle-of-the-road Eurovision song contest. Not for this group!

Like the Slits, the Mo-Dettes got to work with reggae and Lover's Rock producer Dennis Bovell, whose dub section was key to the track's appeal. "I learned a lot from Dennis, but the track was barely us. No way to re-create it live without a couple of keyboards," Korris laments. "At least the record company got that we weren't going on Eurovision. Their manipulation was evident from the start. Did they think we would be more naïve because we were girls? Despite the champagne provided at signing, I sat and read the damn contract through"—what, no lawyer?—"and we caught these points: along with relinquishing the creative control they had verbally promised, they tried to sneak in a pregnancy penalty. I don't think parenthood clauses are injected into recording contracts written for men."

* * *

The dreaded possibility, for some record companies, of new life messing up the marketing schedule happened to Neneh Cherry, the ceaselessly innovative Afro-Euro-US artist. Her "Buffalo Stance" is poised on the volcanic edge where punk, rap, and reggae sizzled together in the early 1980s, when the teenage Cherry soaked up all its young heat. In the midst of recording *Raw Like Sushi*, the album on which "Buffalo Stance" appears, Cherry discovered that she was pregnant with her middle child, Tyson McVey, who, like her other daughters, Naima and Mabel, would grow up to be a musician. Cherry informed her label head at Circa Records, Ashley Newton (father of DJ Harley Viera-Newton), of the pregnancy. "He never told me not to do it, but Ashley had a very confused look. I just said, 'It's going to be fine,' and in fact, it was like it was meant to be that way. I found it empowering because I did not let it stop me, and it became something beautiful rather than bad."

The musical royalty into which Cherry (and her musician brother, Eagle Eye) was born included jazz legend Ornette Coleman, her "uncle"; percussionist Ahmadu Jah from Sierra Leone, her father; and Moki, her multimedia artist mother, whose clothes and stage design helped create much of the colorful ambiance around the stepfather who raised Neneh, the harmolodic trumpet player Don Cherry. The primary link between Neneh's avant-garde bohemian background and punk came with the witty wordsmith Ian Dury, another punk iconoclast; steeped in jazz, he invited Don Cherry to play on tour with his band, the Blockheads. Then fourteen, Neneh came along and met the Slits, who were also on the bill. Swept up as *sistr'en* in the tornado that was the band's lead singer, Ari Up, Neneh joined them for two years. She then became part of post-punk's ferocious Rip, Rig and Panic. Along with fellow singer and dancer Andi Oliver (later to become a celebrity chef and restaurateur), Neneh and then husband Bruce Smith, who drummed with both bands, stormed through passionate harmolodic punk-funk.

Cherry now lives between Sweden, Spain, and London, making searing, minimalist contemporary music siphoned off from her personal gas tank of pain and joy; its poetry is poised between the dance floor and the avant-garde. Also acting in movies, Cherry is a harmonic convergence in her own right. At the turn of the twenty-first century, her deeply humanist "7 Seconds," co-written in 1994 with her second husband and singer/producer Cameron McVey and her duettist, Senegalese griot giant Youssou N'Dour, was voted Song of the Century by the nation of France. But she had already become a star in 1988 with the punky B-girl charisma of "Buffalo Stance."

"It was all about the time and place you were in *right then*," Cherry stresses of the immediacy and urgency of the time she grew up in the arts, starting as a young teenager in the late 1970s.

"I'm a mishmash of different things, a potpourri of stuff. When I came out of being in Rip, Rig and Panic, I started to find my own identity, having come up in New York and Los Angeles and Sweden, then coming to London when I was sixteen. That is where I discovered more of the old school reggae culture— *youthmen*," added the writer and singer of the powerful song "Manchild." "Conscious roots, reggae's voice of revolution and activism, is really important." (Disclosure: as a young writer for the UK music press, I was swept up in the Cherry hurricane. Moki Cherry showed me one could be an artist and still have a home life, and Ari Up, Neneh, and I sang behind artists like

Prince Far I for dub producer Adrian Sherwood; we would dance all night to sound systems in reggae *shebeens*, after-hours clubs.)

"The beauty of the connection between punk, reggae, and hip-hop was that you could be a part of it. But the most important ingredient was finding yourself and having your own voice. You had to write your own rhymes. 'Buffalo Stance' is very much about non-conformism," says Cherry.

It is a fairy tale for any song—the little B side that could, becoming not just bigger than the main track, but one of the key songs of its time. With her sunrise smile and profile befitting a goddess on an ancient coin, Cherry had been seized on as the cool chick in the "Buffalo" style and music posse centered around the stylist Ray Petri. An innovator who made *The Face* magazine the zeitgeist-defining visual force it was, Petri and his team, including stylist/jeweler Judy Blame, had an image of a new, inclusionary ragamuffin-mod look rooted in an updated James Dean 1950s aesthetic of straight-leg Levi's, a white T-shirt, and an ex–US Army bomber jacket, which soon became a clubland uniform for girls and boys. Glowing and beaming, Cherry sealed a moment when she appeared on the cover of an early *Face* magazine—and entered herstory promoting "Buffalo Stance" while pregnant on television's *Top of the Pops*, wearing a tight miniskirt over her bump and getting *down* . . . the first artist ever to do so.

"When we did the track, we didn't think about it too much," she says. "The original version was actually the B side of 'Looking Good Diving' by Morgan McVey."

Who's that gigolo on the street
With his hands in his pockets and his crocodile feet
Hanging off the curb, looking all disturbed . . .
That's the girls on the block with the nasty curls
Wearing padded bras sucking beers through straws
Dropping down their drawers, where did you get yours?

By the time Cherry first cut "Buffalo Stance," she had already divorced Smith and become a single mother. Now embedded in the Buffalo posse, she was involved with McVey. The clean-cut singer-songwriter's duo with Jamie Morgan, called Morgan McVey, was initially the main attraction. All three traded ideas for a more streetwise flip side, contributing lines and verses. But the song's full flavor represented Cherry, with its vibe of hustling in New York or LA, both cities in which she had lived. Homegirl fire as real as her oversize, faux-gold hip-hop earrings flashes in Cherry's eyes as she crisply utters, "Don't you dare mess with me" in the video, then switches smoothly from heartfelt singing to smart rapping in a cod Cockney accent ("What is he like, anyway?!" a favorite catchphrase of clubrunner and DJ Fat Tony.)

"We did it because Cameron and Jamie were out doing PAs [personal appearances to backing track] to that tune, and they were wanting to have something else more clubby and with attitude," she recalls nonchalantly. "I went in the studio with DJ Milo and Nellee Hooper [producer of Bjork and Bristol's Wild Bunch, and Massive Attack co-founder], and we cut "Buffalo Stance" in a few hours. I've always liked that punk mentality, playing with the conventional 'isms,' turning things 'round."

Cherry's assertive voice lit up a track that already blazed fireworks. Bomb the Bass, a.k.a. DJ Paul Simenon, was a local hip-hop artist with a cartoon imagination and a witty approach to his mixes and flow in the innocent early days of hip-hop, when scratching records was still a novelty. He picked up and dusted off the little throwaway B side and brought Cherry back into the studio in 1988, where they sampled a riff from "Looking Good Diving," then re-recorded the whole thing to a track that shakes like a maraca with surprises.

She freestyled the vivid spoken section, "When your shoes worn through and there's a rumble in your tummy," and the snappy, emphatic intro came to her as she bopped to the corner store: "WHO's that gigolo on the street with his hands in his pockets and his crocodile feet?" Immediately, she conjured up not grey, damp London, but sweltering New York nights on fire escapes in Alphabet City, or the front porches of Compton, LA, as kids tested their wiles and styles on the streets. The story is age-old, but as in Chrissie Hynde's "Precious," the finale remains unresolved. Mr. Crocodile Feet is looking for fresh meat for his girl-peddling operation, and the protagonist is skeptical. But that's when Cherry suddenly sings her own words, with lyrical poignancy, "No money man can win my love / It's sweetness that I'm thinking of."

"It is a love song, but in a funny sort of way it's a love song to yourself. A lot of love songs from the female point of view have a dependence riff—I'm always waiting for you. But this is positively defensive, more of an anthem celebrating fitting into your own shoes," Cherry says.

And the record found its own feet, all by itself. "I went out touring with Bomb the Bass," Cherry remembers. "We had three backing tracks and Gilly G (their friend) emceeing. 'Buffalo Stance' was one of them. It was a small tour, but people started to recognize the track. And then it started flying." The unknown artists' tune hit number three on both the American and British charts. "It's one of those tracks. It's a blessing to have a few of those in your life along with the musical journeys."

But it was an intense time for Cherry, signing her first contract, having her second child, making her first solo LP—and looking after her mentor, Ray Petri, who was dying of AIDS. As they sat together in Soho Square one day, Ray said to her, "I am on my way out. I think a new life must be right."

"That is what my core has always been; my life story is the fact that I had kids young and we lived the way we lived, quite communally, making music together," says Cherry. "At the end of the day, that's worth a lot more than money."

Punk love can often be an abrasive saga, involving negotiations within gender wars and power plays, asking if sacrifice is necessary for an autonomous creative life. In these songs, women work through a lifetime of seeking connection. We seek to understand our erotic drives and how to unleash them when female flesh, especially young meat, is a commodity that a predatory entertainment business must refresh as regularly as vampires seek new maidens. Marriage may be seen as a deep collaboration or an unfair trade-off, but the urge to merge remains. If your genetic family cannot follow where you need to go, punk love means gathering a tribe, some maybe unprecedented form of community. Gender liquidity has also impacted the minefield of girls' mores by jiggling the boundaries. Instead of simply asking what makes a girl and boy fall in love, the question has also become, What makes a girl a girl, or the reverse? If you don't recognize yourself, love is harder to find; you don't know who might fit. Until you try.

LINEUP & TRACK LISTING

1. Pragaash (India, 2014).
This Indian teen girl trio were banned by a cleric's *fatwa* and never got to record.

2. The Vinyl Records, "Rage" (India, 2017).
Reinventing new wave, Indian style; raging anti-oppression lyrics delivered with infectious hilarity.

3. Sleater-Kinney, "Little Babies" (US, 1998).
Clever Riot Grrrls question gender roles in surfy pop-punk.

4. Zuby Nehty, "Sokol" ("Falcon") (Czech Republic, 1997).
Eastern Europe's punks were more musically sophisticated rebels, often banned by the authorities . . . Zuby Nehty's sisterhood soars.

**5. Las Vulpes, "Me Gusta Ser Una Zorra"
("I Like Being a Bitch") (Spain, 1983).**
This primordial girl punk band shocked staid Spain.

6. The Selecter, "On My Radio" (UK, 1979).
Pauline Black and her 2 Tone ska band's wit and zip charmed an often hostile media.

**7. Vi Subversa/the Poison Girls, "Persons Unknown"
(UK, 1981).**
Anarcho-punks created a Brighton community and challenged the British government's Irish war with commanding insight.

**8. Jayne Cortez and the Firespitters, "Maintain Control"
(US, 1986).**
Searing indie African American artist, activist, poet, and publisher dismantles the structure of social oppression in a harmolodic song.

**9. Tanya Stephens, "Welcome to the Rebelution"
(Jamaica, 2006).**
A thrilling call to not only dance but make change from an outspoken, controversial independent artist.

10. **Sandra Izsadore with Fela Kuti/Afrika 70, "Upside Down" (US/Nigeria, 1976).**
    The Nigerian creator of the influential Afrobeat sound, Fela Anikulapo-Kuti, wrote this tough critique for his American Black Panther muse to sing.

11. **Skinny Girl Diet, "Silver Spoons" (UK, 2015).**
    London sisters plus cousin lacerate ingrained class privilege over kinetic industrial electro-punk.

12. **Fértil Miseria, "Visiones de la Muerte" ("Visions of Death") (Colombia, 2005).**
    Since 1990, the Castro sisters of Colombia's Fértil Miseria have used punk to challenge anguish and anger. It's a track on a knife-edge.

PROTEST

Woman the Barricades

Now our slogan must be: comrade women workers! Do not stand in isolation. Isolated, we are but straws that any boss can bend to his will, but organized we are a mighty force that no one can break.

Alexandra Kollontai, "Our Tasks," 1917

"WE HAVE TRIED. You cannot have a girl band in Kashmir," the young Indian singer and guitarist Noma Nazir states flatly, her face carefully expressionless. As the local TV interviewer presses her about why she has decided to stop her fledgling band Pragaash (Light), which had been building a following, she looks increasingly ill at ease. The granite weight of centuries of tradition seems to press on the hapless teen's vocal chords, preventing her from the sort of outburst cherished by punk. Flatly, she recites what sounds like a fake statement read by a kidnapped hostage. Before she almost runs away from the camera, Nazir stammers in fear, ". . . a *fatwa*." A death threat had been issued against the band by the regional Muslim authority, Grand Mufti Muhammad Bashiruddin, who declared the band "un-Islamic" under Sharia law.

Nazir, drummer Farah Deeba, and bass player Aneeqa Khalid had simply decided to form a punky girl trio, and they found mentorship in a local label. The ninth-grade students had been hailed as hopeful beacons for cultural renewal by local TV in

2012, delighted to broadcast the trio playing *tablas* (drums) alongside rock guitar. An oft-disputed region and the only Muslim state in India, Kashmir had been split between India and Pakistan at Partition in 1947 and was still trying to recover from its most recent decade of fighting. Reviving the traditions of music and dance that, along with its mountainous beauty, had given Kashmir its mystique was a regional priority. Cut to two years later and the fatwa. Pragaash are receiving online threats of rape, despite support from the chief minister of Jammu and Kashmir, Omar Abdullah, who tweeted, "I hope these talented young girls will not let a handful of morons silence them." Sadly, the girls did indeed shut up, deciding that being in a punk band—having freedom to play, their way—was not worth the risk. The unassuming trio, who performed in modest clothing with covered heads, were now eager to return to their engineering studies. Obviously, sacrifice was not what they had signed on for. Yet, despite Nazir's stoicism, there was a wistful resignation to the set of her shoulders as she walked away from the camera and away from her creativity—at least for now.

Exceptionalism can be exhausting. The very existence of girl punks, the serious/hilarious kind, is evidently a litmus test of a nation's liberality and admiration for rights like freedom of speech and artistic expression. The viability of girl punks in Mosaic religions is questionable. In some strict Islamic movements, though the sound of the recited Qur'an is melodic, music itself is *haram*, forbidden. Every ritual moment is drenched in music, but the strictest Orthodox Judaism bans men from hearing women sing, resulting in female-only choirs (if not, as yet, punk bands).

However, the secular world is also bound by gender. These women all have their own front line—national, global, or domestic—and use punk as their weapon. Barrier-busting is their default mode; had they not created their own channels, in most cases, they would never have been heard. For some in civil war zones, their shows are vital local lifelines where supplies are gathered for hungry kids. Stereotypically, arty types are ditzy and not good organizers, but it is not always so. A hallmark of some of these artists' activism is the creation of a tribe, an extended (if not actual genetic) family. What might seem just a friendly little local scene can resonate for centuries, like Dada, which started in a small Zurich cabaret nightclub in the 1920s. In the absence of old-school access to the mass market, a niche or a new media platform can eventually sustain an indie empire; a festival or conference can urge or ignite a movement. Sometimes, so can a silenced song.

The thwarted teens of Pragaash became international news. Stopping them from making music was understood to be a touchstone for human rights, which, like democracy, are sometimes seen as quite a rich world concept. Indeed, the Mufti thundered about "westernization" and accused Pragaash of being part of a process of liberalization, which he claimed had led to the sharp rise in abuses ranging from mass rapes to acid thrown in women's faces to the trafficking of child brides in the mountains of Pakistan. *The Guardian* reported, "[The Mufti's accusations] outraged many who believed . . . sexual violence is the result of deep-rooted cultural misogyny."

* * *

Swathes of the world are locked in a culture war between the more cosmopolitan urban centers and the "underdeveloped" areas. Even in a major city such as New Delhi, pop-punk band the Vinyl Records are aware of the fatwa imposed 577 kilometers away. "What happened with Pragaash is the reflection of the patriarchal mindset of the society. All these horrors of everyday rape, domestic abuse, and murder in our everyday newspaper (some unreported) affect us deeply," note the Vinyl Records, speaking as a band.

> Be it Kashmir or Delhi, we are still not safe. The list of don'ts is too long for us to go into here. Violence and

injustice against women has its own harsh history. Sadly, even after all these years of revolution and modern advancement, we are still stuck with the differences in socially constructed gender roles, and it's a major barrier to overall human development.

We were young kids playing music after our college hours (sometimes we did bunk)! We were happy being a part of the indie music scene, which was much more organic back then in 2011.

More recently, increased acceptance brought gigs with corporations like *Rolling Stone* and Red Bull. Within the big business of Indian music, the Vinyl Records are young upstarts who, in a positive twist on the often angst-ridden topic of cultural appropriation, developed their '60s-inflected, urgent pop-punk/new wave by listening to Western pop that they discovered, internalized, and made their own—especially music made by girls. Their upbeat sound belies the tough words of "Rage."

> Misogynist fuck
> Is this the best you've got?
> I don't fit
> In your grave
> Go get covered up in dirt

Over a giddy mash-up of textures urged on by stomping bass, the girls sing of revolution, breaking into delirious drama, shoving away harassers with cries of "How dare you, asshole!" "Get out of my face, motherfucker!" and triumphant laughter. It's far from the lush arrangements of much Indian pop. The Vinyl Records have the fortitude to continue, an island of punk in a Bollywood string section sea, strengthened by support from their family and home team, and the audience they have built independently online. That confident narrative is reinforced by the video for their satirical song "Ready, Set, Go!" about their home town, in which the Vinyl Records, dressed in zany mod gear, talk their way into an uptight uptown party and take it over; indeed, bands that look like them are starting to appear in India.

"We are not sure if we are the only official female punk band in the country," the Vinyl Records reflect. "Every quarter or two, we come across some female musicians and bands in some part of the country, which is a very good sign."

* * *

As the second decade of the twenty-first century progressed, a curious case of the era's obsession with cultural appropriation began to happen. Tastemakers in the rich world wanted a piece of the punk action and began to co-opt the punk sensibility. It was not just the usual designers of expensive clothes, but even right-wing anti-abortionists who began to look and sound like punks (if you didn't listen to the words). Equally, there has been a cynical backlash against punk, for various reasons. It started with resentment toward the numerous fortieth-birthday celebrations orchestrated by the same British government bodies who had tried to ban it at its birth; toward the breezy way people are called "punk" just because they wear a tartan miniskirt, a tattoo, and a nose ring, even if they play pure pop; and equally, because the tropes of punk style—those transgressive animal prints, fetish wear, and neon that original punks had to assemble themselves from jumble sales, older adult's closets, and thrift store finds— have indeed been commodified, available by the rack at your local mall. Some say punk music is kaput, castrated, with no place in today's struggles. That elitist view is usually held by blasé metropolitans or disgruntled ex-punks on a pension, those with the luxury of time to overthink things and the tendency to ignore what goes on beyond their own, sometimes privileged purlieus.

Punk is still on the barricades. In Indonesia, punks had their mohawks publicly shaved and were jailed; in Russia, Pussy Riot's art-punk activism sent them to remote, brutal prisons and a life of harassment. Even on New York's Lower East Side by Tompkins Square Park, where the homeless made their 1970s tent city when punk was brewing in those tenements, a punk band *with a permit to play* (not a nicety one would have observed previously) was beaten up for no reason by the police in 2017. Authoritarian regimes understand that punk's quintessential raw primitivism is a threat to their control. In its purest form, it represents empowerment, enabling people without access to talk back to the dominant power structure and make their own statement with sound. Very often, it will be loud and angry—especially for girls, among whom the volume may be softer, but no less furious. They know that despite years of struggle, they are still paid less and have less access to power and control over their lives, that with inevitable passing years more people will attempt to diminish their influence—and it is maddening. Punk means outrage toward rapacious capitalist and/or neoliberal systems. Punk means that women have the right to decide the fate of their own body. Crass chronicler Richard Cross speaks of "the sub-cultural expectation of co-operation and self-activity." These beliefs are the nonnegotiable heart of punk, and it is intrinsically a music of resistance against those who think otherwise.

But how to delineate the quickly shifting boundaries on the map of human social relations? A key tenet of second-wave feminism in the 1960s was "the personal is political," and that doesn't change. Feminism frequently critiques supposedly "female" roles in the domestic sphere. One of the neatest dissections of our traditional duties comes from Sleater-Kinney, whose clever, edgy rock made them one of the more commercially successful of any punk bands. Even for Sleater-Kinney's broad sonic and emotional range, 1998's "Little Babies" is unusual, with its surfer girl feel and '50s harmony group inflection, coupled with Corin Tucker's tightly controlled vibrato.

I'm the water I'm the dishes I'm the suds
I will comfort, make you clean, help you cope
When you're tired feeling helpless
Come inside I am the shelter
And then when you're feeling better I'll
Watch you go

Carrie Brownstein has acknowledged her gratitude to Kathleen Hanna, Bikini Kill, and the first-wave Riot Grrrls with their third-wave feminism for hacking through and creating a clearing in the patriarchal jungle, enabling groups like her own Sleater-Kinney to operate. Co-founded with another of Brownstein's sheroes, Corin Tucker, who had been in the duo Heavens to Betsy, the band were soon taken up far beyond their Olympia, Washington, environs.

"Little Babies" comes from their 1997 album *Dig Me Out*, which in part chronicles the break-up of the two women's own romance. The song's lyrics, though, without the tongue-in-cheek delivery and blithe tune, offer a fascinating duality. They can also be read as a primer for parenthood, developing a nest from which children can fly strongly when they are ready; in fact, unconditional love seems to be what Sleater-Kinney mock when, after listing elements of the domestic grind, they conclude that after facilitating everything for the loved one, the loved one always leaves. It is impossible to say everything in one song, obviously, but let's not forget an interesting corollary: shown proper love, children who split the nest will fly home again. And lovers? If the connection was true, they can turn out to be friends for life, too, as Sleater-Kinney's women went on to prove.

The problem is not essentially with the work of caring itself, the humble domestic chores that the Sleater-Kinney song understandably satirizes. As has been discussed since before the dawn of feminism, the issue is that women so frequently wind up being the ones expected to do it all in much of the world (excluding sensible Scandinavia), and without pay. No wonder resentment builds.

But the fact is that somebody does have to do it, be it a parent, grandparent, foster parent, au pair, elder sibling, or distant uncle. A theme of Riot Grrrl alienation and anger stems from having been denied their childhoods, precisely because they were deprived of what Sleater-Kinney sing about sarcastically: a home base that is nurturing, giving them the strength to develop and grow. With an absentee mother and an emotionally distant father, Carrie Brownstein is a true poster child of the Riot Grrrl tribe, many of whom appear to have been parented by self-absorbed narcissists who didn't want to be there. They never managed to take on board the reality that at some point, good parenting may well involve sacrifice of what one thinks one needs, to earn its many joys. Happy families are not easy to pull off, but luckily they can take many forms—including a violent street gang (not advised) or a radical punk community (far healthier). Effectively, some of those un-parents left the work of helping their children grow to the Riot Grrrl movement. Brownstein writes in her 2015 memoir, *Hunger Makes Me a Modern Girl*, "Sleater-Kinney were my family." As bell hooks writes in her book *All about Love: New Visions*, "The extended family is a good place to learn the power of community . . . if there is honest communication between the individuals."

Dig Me Out was recorded on a tiny budget over ten freezing days in the winter of 1996. Some of the time, the band stayed at Brownstein's father's place; although he was, Brownstein adds, "hard to know and gave little indication there was much to know," he was the constant in her life. And for the first time, she even spent a couple of nights at her mother's, whom Brownstein had rarely seen since she left when the girl was very young. Every child deserves nurturing, and Brownstein knew she had been betrayed. "We want our parents to be the norm from which we deviate."

Brownstein recalls discussing the meaning of certain of their own songs with Corin Tucker, including "Little Babies." Their debate is about whether those feelings were directed at one another or at their needy fans. For Brownstein, who went on to become a multiple award winner as writer/producer of hip TV shows like *Portlandia*, it begs many questions about how a woman performs on stage and about her relationship to her audience. Both women appear to regard their songs as literal descriptions of actual events, quizzing one another about which individual might have prompted certain lyrics.

* * *

Coming from their confessional West Coast culture, the long-running Sleater-Kinney often view songwriting quite differently from the guarded, coded approach typical of musicians used to being spied on by government informers, like fellow veterans, the Czech band Zuby Nehty (Tooth and Nail). Quizzed about the meaning of their 1997 recording "Sokol" ("Falcon"), singer Pavla Jonsonnova explains kindly, "It is not literal. It is more existential."

The song was written by fellow band member Marka Mikova about a captive boy called Sokol, as she was thinking of the bittersweet freedom that followed her children leaving home—the natural end result of parenthood, and precisely what Sleater-Kinney's song disdains as invalidating the effort of homemaking. At the same time, the lyrics obliquely suggest being constricted in your freedom of movement by an authoritarian regime.

> He stands in front of the house . . .
> Then he waves up, come down
> I'm locked here
> I cannot go anywhere
> Outside the heavy snow falls
> He cannot go anywhere

Though mating and parenting could have disrupted Zuby Nehty's career, the five women found a way to keep going, helping each other. "We kidnapped the children to rehearsals and performances, and it somehow worked miraculously," says Jonsonnova. "We still had the desire to have a band based on friendship."

For all punks, male and female, in the former Czechoslovakia, the freedom we associate with the genre was not a right. That knowledge was engrained by the fateful 1976 meeting, eight years after the Communist invasion, between activist dissident playwright Vaclav Havel and the prankster jazz free-funk band the Plastic People of the Universe. It soon resulted in many of the musicians being jailed. The Plastic People also became counter-cultural heroes for their engagement alongside Havel and others with the subversive manifesto *Charter 77*. Though banned, the mission statement became an inspiration for the 1989 Velvet Revolution led by Havel, whose eventual presidency seemed to signal change. But by having a group of close girlfriends, the five women of Zuby Nehty have out-lasted every form of leadership for three decades.

Their bond helped them surmount formidable institutional challenges quite different from those faced by Sleater-Kinney. Notes a New Yorker with a long history of promoting Eastern European punk, Bryan Swirsky, "Thinking about Eastern European music, keep in mind: concepts of free speech did not exist in these countries for many reasons. Mainly, protest was banned in most countries and anyone who went public against the state found themselves harassed by the authorities. During the 1980s, it was mostly men rather than women who were put in prison for their political views."

Underground groups of dissident musicians included punks, who identified with the British and American musicians of the time. That special Eastern European brew of mad technique with punky outrage buzzes on "Sokol": a more orchestrated and sophisticated post-punk, punctuated by unpredictable breaks and tricky structure and harmonics. With a controlled, subtly ironic vocal delivery, Jonsonnova glides through epic arrangements that veer abruptly into a polka-beat section swathed in misty jazz flute, then build to a punk frenzy of scratchy guitar. Unlike almost every other band in this book, Zuby Nehty are experienced musicians: Jonsonnova had ten years of keyboard studies, including three years of organ and theory, at the People's Music School. Sax and flute player Katerina Jircikova studied music at Charles University in Prague.

She stands in front of the house . . .
Then he waves up, come down
I'm locked here
I cannot go anywhere
Outside the snow falls snow
She cannot go anywhere

The waves of grudging governmental tolerance of dissident underground music hit low tide just when things were looking up for the group; they were offered a residency at the Klubko club, a venue approved by the SSM (the *Socialistický svaz mládeže*, or Socialist Youth Union) in the town of Kladno. "It seemed very promising until I was called by a lady from the District Committee," recalls Jonsonnova. "She said our lyrics were too pessimistic and that after reading them she felt like drinking a bottle of wine and jumping off a bridge. She refused to spread such an ideology among the young people of Kladno. It was shocking. I argued in vain that beauty had been a complicated term since the French poet Baudelaire in the nineteenth century. She said she understood that it was much harder to write happy songs, but that until we could, we could not play in Kladno."

"Basically, the hunt against new wave and punk in the first half of the 1980s made practically everyone blacklisted, and the strategy was to change the name and carry on," Jonsonnova shrugs.

"Many things were under the radar; it was impossible to check each and every student concert. It was extremely annoying, but we tried to laugh about it."

So, for a couple of years, Zuby Nehty became Dybbuk, named after the tricky, malevolent undead spirit of ancient Hebrew lore that possesses you at night (a composer friend had read of the Dybbuk in a Joseph Heller book, rather than in the early-twentieth-century Russian/Hebrew/Yiddish play by S. Ansky). After lineup changes, Zuby Nehty met "a wonderful guitarist named Eva Trnkova. She said she had always wanted to play in a girls' band, so it was great," enthuses Jonsonnova. "When five of us stood together on stage, it was a force."

But gender wars were ones they did not have to face. "Czechoslovakia is a small country with a very different background to the USA. Historically, men and women were united against the outer enemy. A country where, under Communism, power was not defined by sex nor gender, but by a Party card," wrote Jonsonnova in an academic paper, "Applying Gender Categories to Czech Rock Music."

* * *

There is more than one way for a band to be banned. Having formed in 1980, Zuby Nehty were officially verboten well before they finally got to record their first album in 1993, then make five more and be anthologized in a "best of" box set. While they were being blacklisted in Czechoslovakia, so were their fellow Spanish punkettes, Las Vulpes, the She-Wolves, on the strength of just one 45: "Me Gusta Ser Una Zorra" ("I Like Being a Bitch").

The more traditional a culture, the more it is threatened by the flashpoint that is female punk. As Spain was emerging from a forty-year dictatorship under General Franco, societal and media pressure soon combined to quash the aspirations of Spain's first all-girl rock band—who happened to be punks. Two sisters, in fact, Loles and Lupe Vázquez, age 17 and 21 respectively, formed

Las Vulpes in 1980. The only all-girl punk band around, they were raised among nine rambunctious musical siblings, two of whom, Niko and Bernar, had their own punk band. The girls soon learned how to make themselves heard. Inspired by UK and US punks, in particular movement godfather Iggy Pop, they were the only women involved in the "Barakaldo Sound"—rough Basque punks like the group Eskorbuto, whose anger spiked in the bleak, violent, smack-addled industrial suburbs of Bilbao on the grittier Left Bank of the Ria River. Their aggression was a reflection of the Basque people's fight for separation from Spain, which had started in the 1930s.

Loles would have loved to play with Niko's band, "but they always kicked me out! I decided to form a punk band, and why not girls?" Finding female players was a problem; at some gigs, the sisters would get Bernar and Niko to play with them—wearing wigs. By 1982, the Vázquez sisters had been joined by bassist Begoña Astigarrgo and singer Mamen Rodrigo. Seeking a "strong, provocative, feminine," name, Loles followed the fashion for Basque or English monikers, riffed on her Latin studies, and found the third feminine declension for "wolf." "I had already done the cover of Iggy Pop's 'I Wanna Be Your Dog'—so, I wanna be a vulpes!" she recalls gleefully.

Before they had even developed a full set, in 1983 a hip music journalist called Diego Manrique booked the band for a live studio session on the popular Saturday morning TV music show *Caja de Ritmos* (*Box of Rhythms*). As is so often the case with continental punks, Las Vulpes, with their lacquered, teased hair, looked more polished than their British or American counterparts. They performed "Me Gusta Ser Una Zorra"—after which their career was kaput.

I prefer to jerk off, alone in bed
Rather than lay with whoever talks to me in the morning
I'd rather fuck with executives,
That give their money and forget about it.

I love to be a slut
Eh, oh, ah, ah, ay ay ay ay ay asshole!

"It was a bit premature," comments Manrique demurely. "The *Caja de Ritmos* program was canceled and the director of programming was fired. The band reached fame/infamy in the Sex Pistols way, and they self-combusted some months later."

There were no "wardrobe malfunctions." But though Generalissimo Franco's forty-year dictatorship had ended with his death in 1975, Catholic Spain was still very—well, puritanical. The Popular Democratic Party protested against Las Vulpes, along with the state attorney general. Newspaper editorials thundered about abuse of free speech and corruption of the youth. Elections were coming, and Las Vulpes had become unwitting pawns in the political battle between the incoming Socialists and the old Franco guard, who denounced the teenagers as front-runners of leftist debauchery and moral decay. The state prosecutor filed criminal charges; Loles spent the next three years in court.

The band did get to release the infamous Iggy cover as a single. "We were cheated," says Loles. "We never received any royalties. Las Vulpes were contracted to do a Spanish tour, but there were protests and most shows were canceled. All that affected us a lot. At the end of summer 1983, we separated. We had only wanted to play. I have always thought that they ended my dream."

Nonetheless, the legend continued. The single became a collector's item. They reunited briefly in 1985; then, eight years later, Lupe was murdered. Finally, in 2003 the rest of Las Vulpes were able to record their original set of songs as an album—the scandal of "Me Gusta Ser Una Zorra" had overshadowed the rest. Loles dedicated it to Lupe, who never got to play them in a studio.

* * *

Prior to the comparatively level, arguably democratic playing field of the post-internet music business, access to the mass media was coveted and heavily restricted. As Las Vulpes show, one TV music program could make or break, particularly because often there was only one music program. However, the climate that heralded Las Vulpes' mid-'80s reunion was created by a new wave of more "acceptable" post-punk women. As many of the first-wave wild girls like Poly Styrene and the Slits' careers waned, a more mainstream-radio-friendly crew came and made a name. From operatic bravado to haute-pop/dance as flouncy as a ra-ra skirt, these disparate women brought a neon audio palette to pop, often riding the then-new machinoid chords of the synthesizer. The very briefest survey of post-punkette female hitmakers who prompted the first "Women in Rock" books would include Europeans Lene "Lucky Number" Lovich, Toyah "I Want to Be Free" Wilcox, and Hazel "Breaking Glass" O'Connor"; the Eurythmics' Annie Lennox; Canadian Martha "Echo Beach" Johnson of the Muffins; and Americans Cindy "Girls Just Wanna Have Fun" Lauper and Gwen Stefani. Their styles differed, but they were all played on the regular pop radio and thus touched the masses.

They were conscious of catching a trend wave with their exhilarating ska-punk, but the Selecter from Britain's Coventry in the Midlands knew they had to guarantee airplay on the few pop stations to cement the foundations of what would indeed become ongoing decades of success. Cunningly, the band concocted a snappy, airwave-ready 45 that was also a satire on the mass media—"On My Radio," sung in 1979 by frontwoman Pauline Black. The stylish singer set a tone in more ways than one. Her silhouette of a man-cut suit worn with a jaunty trilby became synonymous with the 2 Tone aesthetic. One of their first releases, "On My Radio" placed the Selecter in the UK pop canon with its infectious attack on the stultifying state of BBC Radio, then the only game in Britain.

Unlike some bands discussed here, the Selecter, with their bouncy urban ska, were recognized commercially quite fast. "On My Radio" was recorded in the rush of the band's early days, when the 2 Tone movement of racially mixed bands was the vogue. But the main, most powerful media still lagged behind. "The BBC would never play punk or reggae, so this was our roundabout way of giving them something out of the ordinary that they would take as a eulogy to themselves, when it wasn't," chuckles Black.

> Bought my baby a red radio
> He played it all day a-go-go a-go-go
> He liked to dance to it down in the streets
> He said he loved me but he loved the beat
>
> But when I switch on I rotate the dial . . .
> It's just the same old show on my radio

"When we came out, the second-wave ska revolution was A Thing. An obscure musical form created in Jamaica in the 1960s came to the fore, taken up by a certain section of young people who prized punk, the Clash, the Slits, and Bob Marley and the new wave of reggae being made by young people like Aswad and Steel Pulse. We were part of that, playing for Rock Against Racism like Poly Styrene, and we were actually making a point of it; let's break down racism and the 'suss' laws on the street," Black says, referring to the iniquitous legislation of the time that enabled police to arrest kids—almost entirely young black males—for the Orwellian unprovability of "suspicion of loitering with intent." She continues, "We thought that black people and white people with a certain way of thinking, all liking punk and reggae, there's no reason not to come together and to a certain extent be united outside the system. And that's what we did."

After a few years of increased touring and international record deals in the latter 1970s, after the passing of Bob Marley in 1981 and the rise of the more aggressive dancehall sound, the conscious Rasta roots reggae crew spearheaded by the likes of Dennis Brown and trios like Culture and Burning Spear found themselves sidelined by the more generally accessible 2 Tone movement.

It had to be admitted, despite attempts to belittle it by threatened Jamaicans, that the Brits brought something of themselves to the party. If it was not as heavy as the original roots music, it equally had a crispness and bounce that worked well on radio. The zip in its skank reflected the cities whose face was being transformed by the first wave of Caribbean immigrants following the wave of independence in the early 1960s, the ones that came after the war to help rebuild battered old Britain, to do the jobs homecoming heroes could not face.

Newly multicultural Britain was about to wed the two oppressed youth subcultures of punk and reggae that Marley sang about in 1978 as the "Punky Reggae Party." The postcolonial/ imperial pairing became influential, certainly for the punks, who quite frequently recorded their own dub versions (the Jamaican remix style) and covered reggae songs. Its offspring would be 2 Tone's revamped ska. The original speedy music had fit in with the exuberance of independence, and despite the later scene's own very leftist politics, it helped to kick-start a transitional moment when the street-fighting 1970s slid into the Reagan/Thatcher era. An all-woman peace camp arose at the time, protesting the American Cruise Missile nuclear installations at Britain's Greenham Common, and it lasted twenty years. Such voices were not completely drowned out, but the segue into the 1980s saw the pitch change, the dominant values shift, and individualistic material success start to matter more than the fights for equality that had dominated the youth discourse since the 1960s.

Now understood as Britain's first "black music," the girl harmony-based sound of lover's rock groups like 15, 16, and 17, along with the genre's divas such as Janet Kaye and Carroll Thompson, was abruptly nudged aside to make way for 2 Tone. The new sound came with snappy black-and-white packaging of a very New British ska/punk hybrid that all corners of the world would seize on and make their own.

It was impossible for Pauline Black not to be aware of her groundbreaking exceptionalism. "I was shattering the fact that there were very, very few British women of color who meant any-thing in the music business," she states. "There was Poly Styrene, and before her, Joan Armatrading, both of whom were great. I did not consider the same old tropes that a lot of other punk women did, all those London types rubbing shoulders, seeing the Clash. I lived in Coventry and had a job as an X-ray technician. It was different 'runnings.' And are white women inclusive of black women when it comes to feminist rights, or is it separate? Which in my experience, it invariably is; and how that is processed is interesting to me. I had more in common with somebody like Poly Styrene."

They first met when the two were seated together in front of the Slits' Viv Albertine, Siouxsie Sioux, Debbie Harry, and Chrissie Hynde for a famous "Women in Rock" group shot staged by photographer Mike Putland. Black and Styrene looked at one another. "We were both thinking, 'What the heck are we doing here?'" recollects Black, the defiance in her voice indicating that she still remembers her fight for acceptance. Both women were mixed-race when it was still comparatively rare in Britain. To add to Black's confusion, however, unlike Styrene, she was adopted with no knowledge of her heritage by a family who had no concept of a cultural identity for "blackness." Thus, she first heard Jamaican ska on 45s being played by her white skinhead girlfriends during school break.

Britain's regional black capitals, London's Brixton, Bristol's St. Paul, Manchester's Moss Side, Birmingham's Handsworth . . . two years after the release of the Selecter's "On My Radio," they would all be up in flames with anti-police riots. But the full force of the toxicity of Britain's race relations was made painfully manifest when the Selecter played the song on the most coveted, the only TV slot that mattered in England—*Top of the Pops*. Broadcast weekly to a fascinated teen nation, kids would gather around the TV set to tune in to that week's revelations in style and musical matters. Appearance meant a band had arrived. And all artists would gather for a post-set drink in the BBC's VIP

Artists' Bar. Flushed with the success of their energetic performance of "On My Radio," the Selecter headed there—only to be turned away by the "jobsworth" doorman. Hats were forbidden, and dreadlocked Rasta bass player Charlie had his tam. Black, too, was sporting her trademark trilby. The doorman was unimpressed by the revelation that hats could serve a religious purpose. But he was finally willing to let in on her own. Unthinkable.

"In that little vignette, we see everything that was going on then, with black women being perceived as less threatening than the males," says Black. "The *Top of the Pops* people went into overload and frothed at the mouth, and in the end we both got in, but it was symbolic of the times. Nobody really knew what was going on; they had never seen groups like us at the BBC before. For a brief period, they were trying to shut the door after the horse had bolted."

"We were at the forefront of what was considered alternative and meaningful—until people like [smooth white boy pop acts] Duran Duran and Spandau Ballet became 'the place to be,'" notes Black ironically. With her many talents, she still found her way as a musician, actress, writer, and broadcaster. Yet tracing her blood family came to dominate her thoughts. She reached a resolution when, having traced her Ashkenazi Jewish mother to Australia and the surviving members of her late Nigerian father's people to Lagos, Black was embraced by both sides. The result of a liaison when her father was a visiting student, the disgrace and sheer difficulty of having an out-of-wedlock mixed baby at that era overwhelmed the young couple, and Black had been given up for adoption. She found him too late to meet, but her father's final embrace came in the form of a vintage 45, pressed in Lagos, that one of his widows gave her—"The 10 Commandments" by the 1960s Jamaican ska wit Prince Buster, a huge influence on 2 Tone. A circle was cosmically complete.

* * *

Habituated to being an outsider, receiving this record as some symbolic connection to the father she never knew helped Pauline Black make sense of her life, her place in the world, as she continued to make "woke" music. It confirmed that music, any art, can be a bond transcending time and place. Two lifelong artists linked by an aesthetic worked with the same belief in Britain and America: Vi Subversa of the anarchist Poison Girls in Brighton and the African American poet, harmolodic free-jazz performer, publisher, and activist organizer Jayne Cortez in New York. Both women were orchestrators. With time, these multimedia artists grew from den mothers to mentors and were invested with the authority of global village elders. The creation of a viable, self-supporting community is a natural, arguably essential extension of bone-deep punk, whose rage is not commodified but hits hard on the home truths . . . whether that home is effectively your pad, your land, or your world.

Famously, the Sex Pistols co-founder and singer-songwriter Johnny Rotten/Lydon sang of "Anarchy in the UK," but that working-class hero was not an anarchist. The line worked well artistically and conveyed the urgency to overthrow a hide-bound old system that anyway seemed to have collapsed to Britons huddled over a candle in the winter electricity strikes. Lydon was not terribly conflicted about leaving the front lines of the United Kingdom, with its overwhelming demands, and finding a home in California's elite beachside movie-star colony of Malibu.

The serious hard-core rebels within the movement, the anarcho-punks like Crass and Vi Subversa and her Poison Girls, lived it like they sang it. In his The Hippies Now Wear Black blog, Richard Cross defines anarcho-punk values: "A rejection of crushing social conformity; of miserable wage-labor; of war and militarism; and a celebration of freedom, both creative and individual." One way of working to overthrow the system with culture rather than violence was to opt out as much as possible. Seeking to detach himself from Babylonian corruption, the band's only surviving member—with the ironic *nom de punk* Richard Famous—Vi Subversa's partner in work and life, now lives on a remote island.

For Frances Sokolov, a British single mother of two, daughter of East London Ashkenazi Jews, punk signaled reinvention time. In a Superwoman switch, the singer-songwriter of 1980's "Persons Unknown" transformed into Vi Subversa, using punk's inbuilt authority to chuck one's inherited identity.

"Punk took me by surprise. I had already defined myself as an anarchist and feminist well before the advent of punk. The world was based in a permanent Cold War economy and was in the processes of industrial globalization—I craved a world that put the values of peoples' needs before, and above, profit," she wrote in an essay on punk philosophy for the anthology *The Truth of Revolution.*

She had already lived various artistic incarnations, including being a potter, and had been part of the louche bohemian set of London's Soho in the beatnik 1950s. But her beat went on. Sokolov pulled off the ultimate life trick of successfully reinventing herself in every era of her life span, a process helped by her true generosity of spirit. At heart, Vi Subversa was a humanist. Anti-materialism, communal living, post-consumerism, creating a functioning model outside the capitalist system as much as possible—these were not just theories but a way of life for her and her rebel tribe.

"The best bands are 'families.' There has to be a common purpose, and common spirit, or else it is all just show business," asserts Richard Famous. "The core of our band always lived together, and our house was also the center of all Poison Girls activity." He continues, "In general, I never thought that we were a band, but that music, gigs, artworks, writing, and talking were part of our life."

"She was about forty at the time she began singing. In the punks' misfit culture, she didn't get too much flack. Ironically, some members of the Brighton Women's Group who met upstairs were much less accepting," recalls her good friend, the writer, musician, and documentarian Helen McCookerybook, co-director with the Raincoats' Gina Birch of the *Stories from the She-Punks* documentary and author of *The Lost Women of Rock Music*. Agrees Famous, "'Punk,' in its broadest sense, gave Vi the opportunity to find her voice both literally and symbolically. For her, that song was a revelation, and the warmth of the reception it got, from an audience half her age, empowered her. We have been told too many times to count that '"Persons Unknown" changed my life.' It certainly hit a nerve."

The song was the Poison Girls' response to the 1978 case of two young Irish anarchists living in London, Iris Mills and Ronan Bennett—later a novelist and playwright—who were accused of conspiring to plant bombs together with "persons unknown." The flimsiness of the evidence and the young defendants' engaging presence made their charges a cause célèbre, and their trial became known as the "Anarchists" or "Persons Unknown" case. The case was ultimately dismissed.

> This is a message for persons unknown,
> Persons in hiding, persons unknown.
> Hey there, Mister Average, you don't exist,
>   you never did . . .
> Flesh and blood is who we are
> Flesh and blood is what we are
> Our cover is blown . . .
>
> Housewives and prostitutes, plumbers in boiler suits
> Truants in coffee bars, who think you're alone . . .
> Women in factories, one parent families
> Women in purdah, persons unknown . . .
> Wild girls and criminals, rotting in prison cells
> Patients in corridors, persons unknown . . .

Part of the genuinely anarchic texture of everyday British life in the mid-1970s were the unpredictable IRA bombs—although in fairness, unlike urban guerillas today, the IRA would usually let the potential victims know in advance, if possible. (The IRA quite often claimed they could not get through to the authorities from a phone booth.) Anyone who hadn't been caught in or narrowly escaped a bombing knew someone who had. This civil war, the "Irish Troubles" as the British called it, was about a centuries-long struggle for Northern Irish self-determination against British colonial control.

The noted Irish-American author and activist Michael Patrick McDonald, whose award-winning book *Easter Rising: A Memoir of Roots and Rebellion* is a favorite of Patti Smith's, grew up as a young Boston punk following Poly Styrene and the Slits. He notes, "There are as many Brits on that equal citizenship train as there are Irish. The solidarity from England, like the Poison Girls and the Au Pairs, was always huge. We had Elvis Costello and Morrissey of Irish descent. But more than anything, the women got it. After all, wasn't the suffragette movement as British (more, actually) than it was anything else? Suffragettism IS essentially republicanism, that is, the non-American, anti-monarchy, anti-medieval-birthright-privilege kind."

Despite the ever-present risk of drama, discomfort, and sometimes death, plus the knowledge that the IRA themselves could be extremely harsh (their signature gunshot wound, known as "kneecapping," did not kill but maimed for life), a significant sector of the British population was appalled at the centuries of deprivation and suppression endured by the Irish. "We don't torture," the Au Pairs' Lesley Woods sang with bright irony on "Armagh" in support of women IRA hunger strikers jailed by the British, reduced to smearing feces on their cell walls to protest their treatment.

Bennett and Mills' Persons Unknown case became a particular flashpoint. "The idea is that with the vagueness of the conspiracy charges, anyone could be held as a potential suspect," explained Black Flag, the organ of the Anarchist Black Cross organization.

To help pay for the defense against what the band was convinced were trumped-up charges, Poison Girls released "Persons Unknown" as a double A side 7-inch with Crass' "Bloody Revolutions" on the flip. But before the release of the 45, the trial collapsed. Nevertheless, the record raised £10,000 from fifty thousand sales—despite being banned by the leading record retailers. After discussions with Bennett and Mills, the Poison Girls decided to donate their earnings to help set up an Anarchist center in pre-gentrification docklands, Wapping, East London.

"Persons Unknown" was written in one rehearsal/jam and was produced the next weekend by Crass' Penny Rimbaud. "The song is seven minutes long, very not punk," notes Famous. A ceremonial call to arms, "Persons Unknown" is sung by Subversa with rasping piledriver directness. In its near-trance repetition, the song is like being punched where it hurts by the truth, over and over again. As Subversa summons the spirits of all anonymous victims of oppression, the heavy pressure of the rhythm reminds us of innocent sufferers in every century. Her solemn, weighty emphasis when intoning this litany of injustice recalls Jewish liturgy, when the supplicant strikes the left of her chest repeatedly in a steady acknowledgment of faults on the faith's most sacred day, Yom Kippur, the Day of Atonement. It was as if Subversa were driving a stake through the sinful hearts of a corrupt establishment.

A pivotal moment in British punk came when Subversa and Famous broke the lock of an abandoned church cellar that would soon become the womb of punk bands in the south of England; without cheap, preferably free, rehearsal space, bands cannot form and experiment. In early 1977, Subversa was asked to manage Brighton's North Road Presbyterian Church, where community groups gathered. She met with the church elders and agreed on a peppercorn rent for bands to use the cellar, which had been locked up since being used as an air raid shelter in the Second World War.

"Vi was a central player to many of these gigs and bands. As a true anarchist, she supported people with whom she didn't necessarily agree, although she always talked them round to a more tolerant way of thinking," recalls Helen McCookerybook. "Vi believed in people being in bands and lent equipment and band members to anyone starting out. She also mediated in disagreements about the frequent nonpayment of rent for the arches (nobody had any money) and made sure that political awareness was to the forefront of any of the bands that she helped."

Among the various projections onto She-Punks debunked by how Subversa lived her life is that it is not possible to create a home and family plus work with your community and be a strong radical artist. But obviously it is infinitely harder without a solid support system. In Vi's case, like the High Priestess of a matriarchal tribe, she had not solely her female posse but also the trio of men she made music with—who were also the great loves of her life, as she was for all of them. In their personal politics, Vi's immediate family, including her two musician children, Gem and Pete, became a microcosm for a whole anarcho-punk community.

"There were so many vulnerable people around—kids who had run away from children's homes, young people out of borstal [reform school], addicts, and general lost souls," recalls McCookerybook. "Vi was a stabilizing force in the Brighton punk scene and kept a lot of people grounded."

* * *

The word *punk* still meant homosexual or "loser" when Jayne Cortez began her radical mission of using poetry and jazz, a form much loved by 1950s beatniks to drill listeners with complex ideas expressed musically, with the directness and cutting edge of an Amazon warrior's arrow. She literally did "maintain control" as the vocalist with her equally ferocious and free-thinking players, the Firespitters, declaiming lines sharper than a blood diamond over rhythms that rumble and spin like great engines of change.

Tracks like the propulsive "Maintain Control" from 1986 set a template that would be followed by later spoken word artists such as American hip-hop actress/poets Sonja Sanchez, Tracie Morris, and jazzy Ursula Rucker; Afro-punk slam poet Noname; and fiery British poets Kate Tempest and Warsan Shire, who is of Somali descent. Beyoncé performed Shire's cutting verse on her epochal *Lemonade* album.

In whichever direction these women flex their spoken word, they are beholden to originator and scene godmother Jayne Cortez, whose insistent delivery hypnotizes; her lines crack like a whip lashing back at the slave master. Innovator and instigator, Cortez used art to tackle social issues, with a pan-African emphasis, on several fronts. Like Vi Subversa an ocean away in Brighton, from her rent-controlled, fifth-floor walk-up apartment in Manhattan's West Village, Cortez used her art to construct creative revolutions by consciously building a community and showing the placement of the barricades.

> . . . You rush to the job
> And type up the card
> And step up production
> To pay for corruption
> But have no deduction
> To pay for your pension

To see Cortez onstage, imperious in peacock African robes, was to tap into the diaspora. A foremother of punk, she was a woman whose clarity of purpose and creative confidence enabled her to live her life as artist, activist, and woman with the same sureness with which she directed the complex polyrhythms of her band, the Firespitters, the musicians who had accompanied her "teenage boyfriend," as she described to me the man who would become her first husband, Ornette Coleman. Their son, Denardo, was the drummer and musical director for both of their bands.

Reiterating the chorus like a mantra, boiling down an issue to its clear essence with bold precision, she wrings new nuances out of lines even as she repeats them till they are drummed into listeners' minds. She rode the Firespitters' rhythm like a general at the head of her harmolodic army. The sound often called "free jazz" was being developed by Coleman while they were married. Her influence on this sound of freedom is implicit, but she was insistent on their separate artistic paths. When her music was being released on her ex-husband's label, she pointed out, "I would have put out my CD anyhow, though it was nice they asked. Ornette didn't have any idea what we were recording. As an artist, I work every day on my work, and I have produced a number of poetry books and records independently. Luckily, Denardo has the business sense."

Yet Cortez's sound is quintessentially harmolodic; she and Coleman still shared players. "It is very rare and wonderful that I have a group of unique musicians who are also people from my past that I can call," she said.

Harmolodics is the truest sound of liberation—more so than punk, as it refuses to acknowledge the boundaries and dominance of regular rhythm. Instead, often once a more conventional melody and motif is established, the music takes wing, utterly free and yet still disciplined by the need for the musicians to hear one another with an absolute empathy born of rigorous rehearsal. Like the Haitian vodoun goddess Erzulie Dantor, worshipped for being tough, disciplined, very maternal, and still a bold free spirit, it took a poet of Cortez's power to spar with musicians as fiery and quick-witted as these. Her staccato words dance around Denardo's drums. Indeed, together they sometimes sound not unlike Erzulie Dantor's drum-fueled ceremonies.

Cortez's story shows how starting in the most basic of ways, by spreading information among your group of friends, within your sphere, you plant seeds that can grow to fertilize culture everywhere. When very young, Cortez moved to Watts, Los Angeles, with her Filipino mother and African American father.

"I come from two cultures, but my main culture is African. We are from many different areas of the continent, and God knows what happened when we got here and mixed with each other— but really, the blues [I work with] means back to Africa. It has to do with coming to America the way we came here, and what we left behind. It's a searching out of all that." She continued, "We were exposed musically in the community of Watts where I grew up. There were a lot of teenage dances with big blues and R&B bands, and radio stations playing it all. My parents had a fabulous record collection."

Awakening other young artists to their heritage by playing them her parents' library of Latin and American music, Cortez was at the heart of the Watts black arts movement in the 1960s, alongside better-known males like the Watts Poets and the Last Poets. There she befriended Coleman and Don Cherry, his lanky, eager teenage trumpet player with the cheekbones of his Cherokee ancestry. Activism was always the sea she swam in. While still in her teens, Cortez was sent down to Mississippi by the Student Nonviolent Coordinating Committee (SNCC) to report on the elections for members back home.

"I always wrote poetry in a little notebook," she told me in 1979 at the release of the first of her many independent productions, *Unsubmissive Blues*. "When you get serious and become public, that's when you really start. You've found a way to express yourself. You tell your friends about these things you've written, and then something happens. In my case, I went to Mississippi to work in the civil rights movement. That was when the political ideas I had merged with the personal. There was such a rich culture in America in the 1960s, political rallies, places for how I was starting to express myself. Using my own personal poetics, the poetics of black people, the voice, everything all mixed up."

Independently, Cortez and Denardo produced a whole canon of multimedia creativity, including poetry books often illustrated by Cortez's second husband, noted African American metal sculptor and fellow Texan Mel Edwards. "If you truly want to be an independent artist, you have to do what you have to do," she observed. "I started to publish my own work because I wanted to be in full control of what I did. It's nice to have power and more equality. If you live your life like that, you should be able to do the business and the creative, too, because that *is* your life."

Not simply a poet, musician, or publisher, Cortez was an advocate and educator in the broadest sense. A prolific lecturer and the recipient of many grants, including one from the Rockefeller Foundation, she came from a generation when a college education was not a given for African Americans. So it was particularly sweet that Cortez ultimately found an academic home at New York University, where she organized several landmark conferences. As founder and head of the Organization of Women Writers of Africa, she set up the 1997 conference Yari Yari: Black Women Writers and the Future, which drew Maya Angelou, Edwidge Danticat, and many other literary notables. It was attended by two thousand women.

But beyond such remarkable feats was the one-on-one generosity and patience with which Cortez mentored younger writers and musicians, including this one. Contributors to the collection of essays *Jayne Cortez, Adrienne Rich, and the Feminist Superhero* marvel at moments spent with Cortez, in which she knew just how to encourage and help to direct their creativity. A session with Cortez was always inspiring. Enquiring about the current project, suggesting how it could be made extra emphatic or find distribution—Cortez always appreciated younger artists' groping progress towards her profound level of artistic refinement. All who were touched by her felt they were better artists for having been included in the dialectical discourse that was her life.

Her last advice to me came at a vulnerable point. It was the middle of the financial crash, a personal tsunami as the music industry was (de)volving and the venerable commodity of journalism was dropping like a grossly undervalued stock; it seemed I was about to lose all I had, specifically, my home. (Happily, my own tribe, genetic and extended, plus tenacity amid life's never-ending changes, helped save me from that fate.) As a happy birthday party for Coleman buzzed around us in his art-filled midtown loft, Cortez called me aside and looked me firmly in the eye. She took my shoulder for emphasis. "*Whatever happens,*" she insisted in a voice just low enough for me to hear—and I knew what she was talking about—"don't let it slow you down. Don't collapse. You just keep on going." She did not live to see me rebound, but every step I have taken since is guided by that inner strength, which is also the essence of punk: if all that is material collapses around you, you will still somehow DIY or die.

Cortez and Edwards divided her last years between the West Village and the seaside home they built in Dakar, Senegal. Cortez is the only woman to have received the honor of having her ashes spread in state ceremonies there and in Nigeria.

Superficial differences aside, this exemplary artist/activist had much in common with Vi Subversa. They both knew how to give voice to the sufferer by claiming a phrase, toying with it until every tone of a simple yet potent expression had been wrung and its meaning was forever embedded in the listeners' heads. Both commanded audiences for their work throughout their lives and, increasingly, beyond. In addition, they both succeeded in mobilizing communities with their art and shared drive—using culture to make a more just world.

Unpacking her mixed African American and Filipino descent, Cortez found that she identified primarily, primally, with Africa and its diaspora. She was inspired by avatars like the African Orishas and Iemanjá, and woman warriors such as Jamaica's Nanny of the Maroons, who showed her contempt for the British army by swallowing their bullets with her bum.

* * *

Despite its "revolutionary rebel" tradition spread by Bob Marley that excited the Slits, Jayne Cortez, and Alice Bag, Jamaica has a checkered history regarding women and their rights, let alone as musicians. Basically, unless you were the sister or romantic companion of a male artist, or ready to be the latter, it was never easy. None of the various gifted girl singers of 1960s ska were able to maintain a career till their veteran comebacks began, decades on. Jamaica's lone female producer in the 1960s and '70s was the Treasure Isle label's Mrs. Pottinger, for whom singer Marcia Griffiths recorded. Celebrated for her duet with Bob Andy of Nina Simone's "Young, Gifted, and Black," Griffiths sang with Marley's backing singers, the I-Three, alongside his wife Rita and Judy Mowatt, who cut the crucial Rasta female album *Black Woman*. All stars in their own right, they sidestepped the norm. Though each generation has boasted a few exceptional singers, women's careers have always been harder to sustain, and socially outspoken female voices are even rarer.

Violence around music was and remains a brutal reality in Jamaica, where many musicians came from materially deprived ghettos whose youth were manipulated into being gunmen by local politicians doling out survival money on an island with no welfare safety net. Marley himself was almost killed by such "dons" in his Kingston home in 1976. So if artists chose to be circumspect and nonconfrontational, it is not surprising, particularly as women barely had a career without the advocacy of a (male, often lover) producer.

Underlining the contradictions between a legendary rebel and his views on women, I once had a flaming row in a London hotel room while interviewing Peter "Legalize It" Tosh, who sang so indelibly of "equal rights and justice"—the most obviously militant of Marley's original Wailers trio. A hapless DJ friend, Dr. Alimantado, tried to break up our argument as Tosh insisted that men were literally superior to women because women could not carry heavy loads if they worked at a dock. I was enraged at his reductive view of what makes a human strong. Tosh was typically obstinate. The standoff made for an interesting article, but a sad one. In his personal life, Tosh cherished and depended on the women around him. He really was a revolutionary in almost every other way, but he could (would?) never connect the dots. This simplistic macho thinking has helped make the Jamaican industry often unwelcoming to female artists' longevity. An annual supply of cute singers not trying to rock the boys-own studio hierarchy often go on to find difficulty maintaining their careers, unless they develop their own indie system, like Tanya Stephens did.

"Generally speaking, Jamaica is extremely misogynistic, so regardless of who had it worst or how it played out for us, we ALL have it bad across the board . . . in music and every other facet of life AND in every era," agrees the controversial singer-songwriter, who came up in the dancehall era of the 1990s when "slackness" reigned. "We have a culture of silence and false pride which says we're not allowed to be completely honest for fear we might 'make Jamaica look bad.' So even those who have taken on the duties of trying to level the playing field often work in ways adverse to our advancement as females."

Dancehall singers like Lady Saw pushed rudeness as radicalism; but the most sustained note of women's rebelliousness came from Stephens, particularly via her fifth album, released in 2006, *Welcome to the Rebelution*. Her blunt dissections of Jamaican politicians on social media (she ripped one leader as "an awful apathetic human who perfected the art of pandering to the hypocrisy of Jamaicans") boosted her reputation as "difficult"—a time-honored indicator of a freethinking woman who speaks her mind. She says of the title track, "I wanted it to be an urgent call to action done in an almost boisterous fashion to counter all the flack it would have to cut through to get attention."

Her articulation crisp and forceful, Stephens's tone is forthright, hammering lines home on one note, then tensely darting semi-tones above to a quick shriek. Her dynamism is propelled by a minimalist, martial rhythm that orders us to fall in line with her commands.

So I say to you now, the Rebelution is urgent,
Stand before you not as queen, but as your humble servant,
Fake leaders claim thrones without building kingdoms,
Same as the music business in Kingston.
We need to fight for the future, for our daughters and sons,
Instead you're trippin' your brothers, fightin' for crumbs . . .

"S/he who fights and runs away / Lives to fight another day," as Bob Marley once sang. Dealing with constant digs while living and working on a (sorry!) comparatively small island, the ever-forceful Stephens chose to make a tactical retreat in mid-career.

"My withdrawal has been a gradual process. I was never fully a part of the 'in crowd' but as I got older I grew more allergic to the hypocrisy and superficiality of it all so I limit my exposure as much as I can," she writes. "My interactions are now limited to social media, and even that I've now decided to bring down from a boil to a very slow simmer. Familiarity in Jamaica breeds so much worse things than contempt! Things which go against my intention of being at one with the universe. I've learned to take nothing for granted when my own observations of my era have led me to sometimes drastically different conclusions than the popular views!" she concludes.

* * *

The Slits' Ari Up sang about being put on the earth to be heard, not to be liked. Seizing the same self-protective position, Tanya Stephens continues to push, fueled by her admirers' belief in her forthright art, which outweighs the negativity. Though successful, Stephens's beleaguered outsider status in her native Jamaica mirrors that of black punks in both Britain and America, whose

Afropunk movement has a symbiotic, though underplayed, link with the rise of African hip-hop and punky singers like Kenya's Muthoni the Drummer Queen. In a goodly chunk of the world, there are no punky girls; in some cases, like lots of Africa, there is an abundance of superb female singer-songwriters using gripping local styles (or riffs thereon) to express their female-positive views on, say, genital mutilation, including Oumou Sangare, Fatoumata Diawara, Rokia Traore, Nahawa Doumbia, Angélique Kidjo, and Mariam of the duo Amadou and Mariam, from Francophone West Africa alone. An impressive transcontinental crew has followed the continent's mid-twentieth-century pioneers like Mali's Amy Koita Dariba, Egypt's Umm Kulthum, and South Africa's Miriam Makeba (a.k.a. Mama Afrika). That country's Busi Mhlongo could belt a guttural ancestral yodel like the root of the whoops of the Delta 5 and the Slits. But one hybrid music of the time did become colloquially referred to as Africa's punk—the riveting polyrhythms of Fela Anikulapo-Kuti (Fela Kuti), who began to be known outside Africa just as punk was kicking off in the mid-1970s. He made a mistress-piece, "Upside Down," with his *Afrikan-Amerikan* muse, the Los Angelean singer Sandra Izsadore.

The larger-than-life Nigerian *auteur* of the complex, compelling Afrobeat sound became legend for his unique, outsize lifestyle. Master of his universe, in his communal concrete Lagos compound, the Kalakuta (Rascal's) Republic, Kuti would greet interviewers regally wearing only threadbare nylon underpants. He was an utterly confident alpha male. His scathing lyrics blasting the series of military regimes that have controlled Nigeria for the most part since its independence in 1960 made him a popular hero and enraged the government, with tragic consequence. In 1977 London, the Clash's Joe Strummer was singing, "London's burning with boredom," while in Lagos, Kuti's Kalakuta was torched to ashes by the military; thirty-six of the women who lived with him there in a loosely polygamous setup were brutally raped and beaten, and Kuti's pioneering activist mother,

Funmilayo, died from injuries she sustained. But that still lay a year ahead in the future when an African American woman named Sandra Izsadore finally fulfilled a long-cherished plan—becoming the only female lead vocalist to record with Kuti. Had it not been for Izsadore, he might never have written socially conscious firebrand songs like the one they recorded together, "Upside Down," for it was Izsadore who politicized Kuti. They met in 1969, during the months he lived in Los Angeles with his band Koola Lobitos. Experimenting with South American music and jazz, and producing a show for Radio Nigeria, Kuti was then very much the bourgeois product of his highly placed, respectable church and educator family, who were prominent even under colonialism. To him, Izsadore was not just stunning but a political and intellectual awakener. As a young Black Panther, Izsadore had even been jailed. She fed him black power books and he repaid her with not only love but music, pushing her from local supper club gigs singing Burt Bacharach to recording with him in London with Cream's drummer, Ginger Baker, for his *Stratavarious* album. Izsadore led him to make the connection between the colonial mentality that still governed Nigeria even without the direct control of the English; and the oppression experienced by African Americans, descendants of thousands of people shipped from Kuti's own shores with local complicity. And all the while, the electrically connected couple spoke of recording together in Lagos.

By the time Izsadore arrived at Kuti's Kalakuta Republic compound in 1976, the man she had known years back in Los Angeles was living quite differently. He had refined the big band Afrobeat sound; his club, the Shrine, was busy with his significant following and large entourage. His compound was like a village in one rambling concrete structure, and Kalakuta's residents included not just some of the Afrika 70 band's twenty-odd musicians, but also the large coterie of women who sang the call-and-response choruses (twenty-seven of whom Kuti would later marry as a sign of support after the army attack.)

I'm beginning to vex up for this land . . .
Fillings boku road no dey, land boku food no dey . . .
People no know Africa great . . .
Communication disorganize
Patapata . . .
Everything is upside down

"Upside Down" was released in 1977, the year of the Slits, the Sex Pistols, Poly Styrene, and the Clash—and we in London were aware of it. The immediate danger of the Nigerians' hands-on struggle dwarfed ours and inspired us to cope more resolutely with our own corner of postimperial death and rebirth.

"I lived inside Kalakuta for a few months before we recorded. What used to be a family home was now a commune with all of the dancers and employees. It was fun. There was music 24/7 and everyone having a good time," Izsadore remembers. "Rehearsing with Kologbo, the guitarist, I embraced it all as a new frontier, learning a culture I had always been curious about because I was curious about myself. History had taught me very little about myself. I had to go in search of truth for my own story, our story, and I thought if I went to Africa I would get that. And then came the rude awakening. I will always say that what colonialism did in Africa is far worse than what slavery did in America."

Echoing Poly Styrene's cry, "Do you see yourself?" in "Identity," Izsadore continues, "The masses I came into contact with still followed the missionary format of the white, blue-eyed Jesus. When you present it to a child and say, 'This was the holiest person, the perfect man,' and in the mirror they see they don't look like that, it causes some psychological damage."

The unique social experiment of Kalakuta came into its own on occasions like the much-awaited "Upside Down" session. The whole tribe prepared for a long night in the studio, carrying pots of cooked food and mats to sleep on.

Izsadore sings with a husky edge and crisply sardonic enunciation over the hypnotic tug of the rhythm: light-fingered rhythm guitar; deceptively simple just-so bass; the shaky tumble of the percussive beaded *shekere*; sophisticated, talkative horns; and jazzy Farfisa organ. Extending over fourteen churning, burning minutes, the song's caustic analysis of urban decay, the angry plaint of a once-proud city failing fast, had blazing relevance. British anarchists like the Poison Girls and Crass would have been humbled by the real anarchy of Lagos. The postcolonial dream of independence was not playing out as liberty-loving optimists and idealists had planned. New masters seemed to have replaced the familiar pale faces of the colonial oppressor. Engrained general corruption led to violence not only from armed robbers and random police street beatings, but from lack of the basic services—waste disposal, garbage collection, water, power—that governments are supposed to supply in the fundamental social contract. Amid Lagos's rapidly exploding population settled packs of "area boys"—homeless street kids, girls too, fending for themselves somehow, anyhow. They were part of Kuti's army, in which, as he sang, music was the weapon. For Izsadore, the fulfillment of her musical dream meant an opportunity to express her own love-hate with the greatness and tragedy of Nigeria through Kuti's lyrics. Their years of intimacy gave birth to a unique and mordantly acute patois protest song that though obviously African is also literally African American.

"I performed it live at the Shrine and it occurred to me, how will the Nigerian audience accept the fact that I'm up there abusing their country, telling them everything is upside down?" laughs Izsadore. "But Fela had written it for me and I was moving forward with his lead. The people loved it . . . there is still a love for it."

* * *

Indeed, there will always be a love for artists who compellingly sing it like it is, exposing and unraveling the frustrations the listeners face in a song they can't forget. Despite its fluctuating oil-dependent economy, Nigeria was still one of the continent's wealthiest countries, and the pathetic infrastructure seemed to symbolize the weakness, greed, and inhumanity at the military government's core.

Coming so unexpectedly, however, a 2017 infrastructure collapse in prosperous West London—the Grenfell Tower inferno in which seventy-one people died—scorched away any veneer of government caring. The tragedy sent an extra chill down the spines of the members of Skinny Girl Diet, especially as it might have been a scenario from their new song, "Silver Spoons."

The two sisters of the band, Ursula and Delilah Holliday, together with their cousin Amelia Cutler, are a mix of races: the sisters, Anglo-Jamaican, and Cutler, Anglo-Chinese. They describe their music as "feminist punk for freaks and weirdos." Their sound is sparse, tense electro-punk-funk: a feedback-blurred blare of phased drums with an audacious bass that skitters to rarely heard high notes. Their music recalls ESG, yet such is the way of these things that when interviewed, the band reported having never heard of them. Delilah's sneering vocal spits contempt for the sort of selfish privilege that caused the burning of Grenfell Tower, whose tenants were mainly immigrants. The working-class council tower block—"project" in America—was a holdout in increasingly gentrified Kensington. The fire happened because the building had been covered in cheap flammable cladding, just so it would look better for the wealthy neighbors.

Even in a time of unprecedented terrorist attacks more lethal than those of the IRA in the 1970s, the sheer scale and symbolism of this disaster horrified England and bound the West London community tightly together. The blaze seemed to emphasize the message of disdain communicated in "Silver Spoons," especially as the song had only just been released on the band's self-financed and -released album, *Heavy Flow*, with a controversial cover shot of the girls dressed in red-stained white.

The sisters were deeply affected by the fall of Grenfell Tower. They had grown up and still lived in very similar government-funded council housing. Says Delilah Holliday,

> It highlighted the tensions all working-class people are going through right now. I have lived in a tower block for all my twenty-one years. I meet or see someone new every day and live with diverse people, from drug dealers to old people who have been living here since the tower blocks were built in the 1960s. It's a wealth of knowledge and context for my art and songwriting that some posh white boy indie band wouldn't be privileged enough to even imagine. However, I'm also at a disadvantage as I find it hard to accumulate wealth, navigate through society, and get taken seriously and given big platforms as an artist/musician. I wrote "Silver Spoons" four years ago, and the saying "I wasn't born with a silver spoon in my mouth" largely inspired it. However, it's also about being constantly under surveillance by the authorities.

> Police corruption
> Causing no government disruption . . .

> Who's staring at me through that lens
> I don't know
> They run the country
> But I still don't know

Underground heroines in mid-2010s London, Skinny Girl Diet took their name from a get-thin-quick product sold by Bethenny Frankel of the *Real Housewives of New York* TV reality show franchise. Not because they wanted to endorse it; rather, they thought the whole idea of it, in an age when so many young girls suffer from anorexia, was insanely horrible. Singer-songwriter Delilah saw the advertisement on TV when she was fourteen years old and suffering body dysmorphia. "I didn't even know it was a product," she says. "I'd seen horrific images on the internet of women starving themselves, and I realized, this is a bigger epidemic—it's not just me thinking I'm a monster every time I look in the mirror. I want to occupy a space that tells women that perfection doesn't exist. It's all just an illusion peddled by capitalism to keep the machine going. It's beyond fitness; it's a mental thing. I will do everything in my power to stop another female experiencing that self-hatred."

Skinny Girl Diet is a family affair. The sisters started adding punky drum fills to their school jazz band—and never stopped. Says Delilah, "We wrote songs about aliens and mermaids as kids. My sister is the yin to my yang." Agrees Ursula, "We talk telepathically, so it is super easy to make music." They are managed by their artist father, Dan. Growing up as a punk in the 1970s, Dan had gone on to open a venue in the basement of the White Horse, a Hampstead pub. Artists he promoted and/or made flyers for include P. J. Harvey, Bikini Kill, and Huggy Bear. He says that managing Skinny Girl Diet is a natural extension of helping them with their homework, and he still makes art "with a DIY aesthetic."

As soon as Skinny Girl Diet began performing in public, they drew an audience of first-generation punks. When the band began, they had even called themselves Typical Girls, after the Slits' anthem. "Women like the Slits, X-Ray Spex, Kathleen Hanna, Bikini Kill, Hole, L7, Babes in Toyland, 7 Year Bitch, and Alice Bag gave me hope that I wasn't just this freaky goth kid who had militant feminist beliefs that didn't fit in anywhere," says Delilah. "I could occupy a space and create my art." A younger crowd followed, expanding their reach. Nonetheless, on some level, both sisters still feel like outsiders.

"I am very much a lone wolf," says Ursula. "It's a cliché to not feel a part of your generation, but I'm a mixed race, bisexual young woman from a council estate. The most comfortable I have

felt is within the queer DIY punk scene, who embraced us. I want
to start a movement with Skinny Girl Diet so eclectic weirdos
like myself can have a safe place to go."

That's just what they do in their video for "Silver Spoons,"
which they directed with Matt Robinson. The girls are black-
vinyl-clad avengers, fearlessly pelting on their bicycles through
playgrounds and tower blocks like their own to stop crimes
against punky girls by bullies, cops, and pimps in what used
to be thought of as a man's way—by beating them up. Even a
pacifist can understand why.

"My biggest piece of advice to young girls starting out,
whether you have a supportive family archetype or not, is one
word: RESILIENCE, which I have learned over the seven years
I have pursued this project. Be militant in believing in yourself.
Don't think, just do, and everything should fall into place eventually," Delilah concludes. "You have to be radical if you want
stuff to change. From being belittled within the music industry
for being a woman, to criticizing the clothes that you wear, there
definitely is an even harsher judgment that we face. As a female
performer, people often ask me, 'Are you an activist or a musician?' Why can't you be both?"

* * *

Making things happen wherever you are, cleverly circumventing
obstacles based on your class, gender, race—that is also punk's
heartbeat. Ideally, it can be a lens to focus that suppressed or
ill-directed passion, make it blaze and fire up into some practical,
tangible entity. Girls' surging energy can be harnessed to make
electricity that lights up a community, as in the case of Skinny
Girl Diet—often with sympathetic, supportive male as well as
female cohorts. Start your own label; open up a venue where your
band can play; create a fanzine and spread it around.

If people's protest movements are to be more than a brief
feel-good fest, the energy liberated by the crowd needs to be

focused and directed somewhere, not just evaporate in blithering rhetoric and might-have-beens. After the excitement, Occupy Wall Street arguably became a poignant though invigorating memory: a movement that dwindled because it lacked coherent direction. A general lament was that it also failed to produce a singular anthem that might have helped to define it. Yet others, like Colombia's Fértil Miseria, do not have to quibble about punk being passé; they use it every day as both sword and shield, and they see how it helps people to face and deal with their lives. In the heat of cultural battle, the needs of distinct groups—even whole ethnicities, or women collectively, or transgender folk—may have to (temporarily, hopefully, unless the war lasts forever) be subsumed into the broader fight of everyone. So it is with Fértil Miseria.

For some black-leathered rich-world downtowners, punk means getting off your face and into trouble with your mates, an escape into a teenage perma-dream, a helter-skelter ride on the oblivion express. They won't mind being labeled as the decadent face of punk; in fact they will relish it, and it certainly has its fun side. But there is another, more survivalist aspect to punk that has helped it to endure as the mouthpiece of revolution. The Riot Grrrls spread their revolution organically, girl-style, in an exemplary fashion. Punks slept on fans' floors, calling out to the audience for a sofa to sleep on as they finished their encore.

But what if your whole country is in a literal state of war and immediate revolution, even beyond the constant killing that plagues America in particular—when the body count is not from opioids or police shootings but from battling militias funded by drug gangs who are both fighting and fronting for world governments, the police, and the army? What does music, punk in particular, mean then?

Via email and with translating help over the phone, Fértil Miseria communicated several times about their song "Visiones de la Muerte" ("Visions of Death") and its video. They even kindly held a special group meeting; the following are collective answers unless otherwise stated.

"'Visiones de la Muerte'" is a reflection of our dread in a society that is full of deep-seated fears and the reality of everyday death. It is the only thing we have for certain," the band states. "The song is also a reflection that we must all one day depart, no matter what we leave behind; it's the pain felt by the families who see their loved ones die with no understanding of what happened. 'Visiones de la Muerte' is everything that we fear; it's the scenes we live day by day, and one can see them reflected back in our video."

> They hit me in the chest, and want me to come back
> And now I do not understand, my mind is floating
> I hear you whisper, "Do not go away, do not die" . . .
> Your parents your family, without you
> Will not be able to resist . . . and I
> No longer want to return

They spell danger, the whirring red lights that fill the screen at the start of the "Visiones de la Muerte" video by director Fernando Puerta. But where did the peril come from? Could be anywhere. Then we are inside the ambulance. Medics are working on a shot man, trying to shock him back to life. At this point, it doesn't even matter who did it. Will he live or not? Next, it is touch and go on the operating table . . . but the kicker is that, at the last moment, the pain of existence so overwhelms the injured man that he is ambivalent about being pulled back to life itself. It's an existentialism that more than rivals the perceived nihilism of Iggy Pop slashing himself onstage.

The Au Pairs in Birmingham made a conscious decision to be a mixed-gender band. The first majority-female band in Colombia, Fértil Miseria, had intended to be all girls but wound up with male guitarist Juan Carlos Londoño because there were no female players to be found.

The band's founders are the Castro sisters from Medellin, bass player Piedad (who also works as a special education teacher) and singer Vicky, a mother who was the region's first female punk singer; both played with other outfits before starting Fértil Miseria. Later, they set up a music shop called Rockandrolltienda as an alternative scene focus. The sisters write, "Our struggle with society began with our family. Mother was a teacher, father a farmer, and they came from a village. They were traditionalists, who never understood rock 'n' roll and thought listening to and playing music was bad. When we began in the 1990s and being sisters, too, we were seen as very provocative. It was partly because we were the first women musicians around, but also because we have been tearing apart this system of shit, pain, and conformism for twenty-eight years."

Their fertile, creative, glorious country of Colombia has been shattered, if not broken, by internal violence manipulated and funded by larger foreign interests, but also enforced by tough local traders in the illegal kidnapping, cocaine, and arms economy. Local wealth includes commodities adopted by the world, including the marinated raw fish dish ceviche, coffee, and cocaine, the weary mountain peasant's friend turned party drug turned international arms trade-off. It can often seem that the more blessed a country is in natural resources, the grimmer its fate, as corrupt local politicians siphon profits into Swiss bank accounts and outside interests lick their lips, vampires happy to drain their victims. For relief, Colombians can turn to their cornucopia of ravishing musical rhythms, such as the *vallenato* and the *cumbia*. However, Fértil Miseria did not turn to their lilting rhythms when they began playing in 1990. Their concerns demanded a harsher expression. They write, "The experiences and the pain we live daily are the main inspirations for our songs but also the hope of a better world." They listened to international inspirations, including Bristol's Vice Squad, Germany's Nina Hagen, Spain's Ultimo Resorte, and particularly New York's outrageous Plasmatics, fronted by Wendy O. Williams, who were known for blowing speakers up onstage.

The Plasmatics' aggressive, full-frontal attack made sense to Fértil Miseria. They write, "The turbulence we've had to witness in this country has been a lot of bombs exploding, wars, violence in the city, running because they were going to kill us."

Over decades, Fértil Miseria have stayed focused on their rebel mission. The band present as nonnormative; in her "wifebeater" T-shirt, tattooed and crop-haired singer Vicky Castro looks tough enough to be a fair-minded butch bouncer: a definite boon on the barricades.

"Fértil Miseria has been around since 1990, screaming with pain, anger at the injustice that is seen in our country. In addition to the drug war we had to live through with Pablo Escobar, this increased scourge of guerrilla and paramilitary factions caused the group of displaced people in our country to grow every day," they write.

"The dying man and all the lyrics reflect the desperation, the fear, the pain, the rage that the people and relatives of victims of violence feel; and even the conformity that leads us to decide that it is better to be dead than to live this crude reality."

Vicky's buzz-saw howl barks out the story over the rock-hard counterpoint of a crisp industrial drum and bass figure, the drummer slashing a tough, tingling hi-hat. The music works like adrenaline on a weary soldier, a necessary energy because at a Fértil Miseria gig, fans and band alike always have to be ready to run from a bombing or guerilla attack, and often don't know which faction might be firing.

"These things have served us in that they've made Fértil Miseria create blunt, aggressive, and challenging music and lyrics. We took our guitars and downloaded all this horror and fear, which is reflected in our lyrics."

The real story behind the song still haunts them all: the four hours in which Piedad and Vicky searched frantically for guitarist Juan Carlos Londoño. Taken from his home by masked gunmen,

Londoño—already a desplazado himself—was bundled into what Colombians call "the car of death" and kidnapped for four excruciating hours. He was one of the lucky ones.

The result is a domestic refugee crisis. Colombia's population of desplazados—also the title of the album from which "Visiones" comes—is the world's second largest.

The Fértil Miseria collective writes,

> As a band, we saw in ourselves a moral obligation to help, and not remain passive in the face of this multifaceted situation. At our concerts, we collect food, toiletries, money, and clothes, which are donated to this group of people at schools, in neighborhoods, and on the streets where many of them live. We also do songs embedded with messages of help that create more solidarity and human consciousness. We feel that these lyrics and music have also led some punk bands to perform other types of actions, such as aid to the environment, animal welfare, etc. As bands, we should not only express our experiences, but also do something for our country and planet.

* * *

Levels of struggle spread before these system-shaking women on the barricades, all crucial. Their battle zone is domestic, professional, artistic, social, financial, political, and personal. From the suburban American kitchen to the food lines of Colombia, civil rights marches to bars at the BBC, these bands have found that punk and other defiant, free-thinking music in spirit are crucial to their solution. Turning art into activism extends the impact of their music. The outspoken defender of "equal rights" Peter Tosh felt that men are superior to women, as many of us may lack their physical strength (not you, O gym rat, yogamatic reader!). But our creativity, as deployed by these artists, is as sinuous and forceful as water, which will shift big cities and wear away mountains.

OUTRO

Our Coda

Let fools fear fate,
Thus I my Stars defie,
(Points to his/her sword/microphone)
The influence of this—must
Raise my glory high.

Aphra Behn, *Abdelazer, or, The Moor's Revenge*, 1676

I BEGAN THIS BOOK asking questions about how girl musicians, often operating outside the establishment system of their day, negotiated their paths through the shadowy forests of the music industry, without the light of a girly herstory to guide them. My thoughts were much with the marginals, those who might never have been able to work in music were it not for punk's open-door, anything-goes, tabula rasa policy established in the mid-1970s. Stroppy, obstreperous, obstinate, unpretty girls wanted to make a sound that startled as much as their appearance; a sound to fling open the patriarchy's windows and let in the light of our real feelings, expressed our way. The generations before us had vied with each other for the attention and refracted power of men. We said—we sang—"Enough of the unseemly squabbling over scraps the gatekeepers might deign to throw us if our behavior and presentation pleases them! We will hunt and gather for ourselves, and cook the stew, too. OK, it's tiring—but at least we will eat."

The tale of punk and women is necessarily one of struggle; it is generally a replay of the old Davida and Goliath story; whether the giant that She-Punks face is the capitalist patriarchy or some form of dictatorship, it is musically fought by all genders together, regardless. The issue of identity posed in the first chapter applies throughout. The original female artists here are all exceptional, not only musically but because they had very few, if any, role models. That suited the punk aesthetic, which is designed for making it up as you go along.

Oh, but we women all found obstacles, from disapproving parents, clerics, or governments, to promoters or radio programmers who will only let one token girl play on their show, to male musicians who act sniffy before you play and jealously undermine you after they hear you're good, to record executives who decree you're too this or that (though never too thin or too young) and producers who want you to pay to play—not even with money. The glorious thing I discovered in unveiling surge after surge of girl strength was how determinedly and creatively these artists have insisted on working, no matter what. Whether it is Pussy Riot in the 2010s, seizing the Moscow streets as their stage, or Malaria! in 1980s East Berlin, jimmying open locked storefronts to stage events where music met art. Punk's DIY ethos coincided with women's necessities.

The fluidity often assigned to female emotions, now applied to the membranes between genders, serves us well in thinking of the connections between punk and girls and women. Punk female music community members are often "absolute beginners," to quote British writer Colin MacInnes. Few are classically trained, other than the Eastern Europeans, and most come up through pubs and bars, the usual punk track. Many emerge through underground ranks, self-invented, first-generation. As I write, a fourth wave is appearing with groups like Britain's Big Joanie; they may still feel alienated, but they benefit from a support system not available to their predecessors. Foremothers like the Runaways' Joan Jett can now cultivate like-minded young bands such as Fea, the Texan Chicanas she co-produces with fellow LA punk pioneer Alicia Velasquez, and release them on her own label. Though every effort has been made by the male-dominated establishment to block the continuity that builds a sturdy creative heritage, there is a push back to relocate women within the nexus of music, such as NPR's attention-stirring list of essential female albums coordinated by activist writer Ann Powers. Others are also joining Chicks on Speed in pulling our family tree together, work I hope to extend with this book's concentration on punk as our first musical liberator.

Naysayers try to deride the release and freedom women find in punk, to diminish it by claiming the genre is played out. But then, those who benefit from an old order also begrudge self-actualized women claiming their own musical agency. The youngest artists in the book, like Hastings' Maid of Ace, still find that punk is the language to help them kick out the negatives in their post-work world.

Retro revivalism has become a standard marketing practice in today's more diffused, less corporate music industry. There is renewed interest in the many women (more than men) who dropped out of making music professionally, feeling not only the lure of the hearth and the challenge of the "next new thing," but the dead weight of institutionalized ageism. As Yoko Ono, Patti Smith, ESG, and Debbie Harry do, brush it aside, ignore it, and make it go away. A fine surprise was discovering how many female pioneers are either still recording or were returning to music as this book was being written. For some, like the Bush Tetras, Köster of Malaria!, and Hang on the Box's Wang, the recording gap has been a decade or more. The expansion of independent music has helped to shatter one of the laddist recording industry's cruel, needless edicts—that a female artist's shelf life is shorter than the next crop of young girls' miniskirts.

In the most politically confrontational communities, where armed fighting is commonplace or music is regularly deployed for resistance, both sexes are often too engaged in confronting their mutual adversaries and would-be controllers to focus on gender wars. Is an actual war necessary for genders to get along? Not necessarily. I also confirmed my suspicion that bohemian, leftist milieus are simply more She-Punk friendly than redneck or orthodox religious zones.

The big question: How did the She-Punks with the least investment in the establishment and the most longevity steer their way through? Some feminist circles like to deride women's traditional nurturing role. But that is throwing the sports bra out with the corset; we all actually do need some support, our own sort of family. In an often uncaring or downright hostile context—or even in a welcoming one—the trick is to throw your art and desires out into the pool of people around you (live or virtual) and work with the ripple effect to create community.

Since the first wave of punks have become grandparents, it has been quite common for female artists to perform with their own musician children—not only Jayne Cortez and Vi Subversa, but Patti Smith, Poly Styrene, Neneh Cherry, Crass' Eve Libertine, Grace Jones, Sandra Izsadore, and ESG—in a generational continuity that may not have been anticipated in the earliest waves of feminism.

The musical mainstream having all but purged the early girls in the 1980s, Riot Grrrls a decade on helped strong, individual musical ladies to step out beyond the system. Now, in the early twenty-first century, one of the biggest stars, Beyoncé (who has recorded in her punk persona, Sasha Fierce), trumpets feminism as she sells her own and others' products. Despite any contradictions, Beyoncé's support has helped to encourage women and create a climate in which people want and can get to hear once-forgotten first-wave originators. The mutual support she and her avant-soul musician sister, Solange, publicly demonstrate affirms how precious consistent closeness can be.

Among the book's revelations for me is the number of bands who embody Annie Lennox and the Eurhythmics dictum "Sisters are doing it for themselves": biological sisters like Beyoncé and

Solange, sustaining each other as they make quite different projects, and actual sisters together in a group. Like the Wilson and Millington sisters of the 1970s groups Heart and Fanny, we have Fea from Texas, Fértil Miseria from Colombia, Shonen Knife from Japan, Las Vulpes from Spain, ESG from the Bronx, Skinny Girl Diet from London, and Maid of Ace from Hastings. That level of emotional investment can help in negotiating the industry's dangerous shoals. Others simply operate like a family, like Zuby Nehty, who insisted on a band based on friendship and have kept it going since the 1970s. Intimacy helps. And when that tribe focuses on turning art into activism, rapids can just move you forward faster.

The devolution of the old-school music industry, in part because of its inability to cope with the internet's ready access, has been a goddess-given gamechanger for women. There is a sense that the weakening of the once-absolute grip of the old Boystown record industry creates an exhilarating space for today's artists—new platforms for new and seasoned voices. As ESG point out, with the old empire crumbling, a more viable environment has risen. But how to seize the fiercely fought over space—beyond being brilliant, of course? Sisterhood of all sorts will absolutely help. In fact, sisterhood saves.

If everything were to be stripped away—electricity, the internet, our phones—what would remain? Only the fundamentals. Even then, I am convinced that there would still be a bunch of wild women sitting on rocks in the dirt around a fire, banging sticks on stones and singing, "Oh Bondage, Up Yours!" And amid the grime and grit, there will be glitter.

ACKNOWLEDGMENTS

AS THE READER CAN DOUBTLESS IMAGINE, even though I had been active in women's punk since it began, it was still a two-year forensics job curating, assembling, finding, and talking to this cast of female musicians. Not only did they have to tell the story of women's changing musical voices and roles in different places and times, but I had to dig their sounds! So let the thanks begin with every artist interviewed here for not only their creativity but their generosity.

For steering me, researching, discussing, and reaching out in many languages: Light in the Attic's Patrick McCarthy and Patrick Sullivan, Maxine Waters, Diego Manrique, Beezer, Daniel Grunenbaum, Jack Tchen, Laura Chen-Schultz, Nathaniel Davis, Ziyi Liu, Bryan Swirsky, Alan Riggs, Paul Bradshaw, Jumbo Vanrenen, Brice Wassy, Gary Sullivan, Professor Kevin Dunn, Krish Raghav, Jonathan W. Campbell, Matt Turner, D. J. Rekha, Evelyn McDonnell, Atsushi Shibata, Sukhdev Sandhu, Mariane Pearl, Judy Cantor-Navas, Miguel Ángel Sánchez Dominguez, Michael Zilkha, Chris Blackwell, Mark Moore, Richard Famous, Ashley Kahn, Jenn Pelly, Meg Handler, Martin "Youth" Glover, Andy Caine, and Alex Paterson. Charlie Waterhouse was most kind to let me read *The Truth of Revolution, Brother: An Exploration of Punk Philosophy*. Please make it available as an e-book, Situation Press people! Also respect to Richard Cross' *The Hippies Now Wear Black: Crass and the Anarcho-punk Movement 1977–84*, George Berger's *The Story of Crass*, and Jonathan Campbell's *Red Rock: The Long, Strange March of Chinese Rock and Roll*. Carlos Boura on Las Vulpes in *Pikara* magazine and

BurningAmbulance.com on Hang on the Box helped me with Basque cultural background. Xenia Grubstein went above and beyond.

Thanks to the once stalwart twentieth-century trio of UK music weeklies, the old "inkies," that did let me into their almost all-male ranks and gave me space to become a writer and music critic: *Sounds, Melody Maker,* and *New Musical Express.* Shout-out to places in which I have been able to explore these ideas, including the *New Statesman,* the *Guardian,* the Alexander McQueen website (thanks, Eve-Marie Kuijstermans), and Chime for Change—Founded by Gucci. The Clive Davis Institute of Recorded Music has given me an academic home since 2005. Professors Beth Denisch and Matt Jenson welcomed me to Berklee College of Music; as did Associate Professor Jack Bratich at Rutgers University.

For the fine thinkers and writers whose concise ideas I quote: bell hooks, Naomi Wolf, Alexandra Kollontai, Dale Spender, Kate Bollick, Gloria Steinem, Chimamanda Ngozi Adichie, Sarah Ahmed, and Aphra Behn, and Angelique Kidjo, who flipped the script on cultural appropriation with her magnificent re-rendering of Brian Eno and Talking Heads' *Remain in Light.*

For my Hat & Beard family, J. C. Gabel, Lara Schoorl, and the beautifully proactive Sybil Perez. Long live Gabel & Goldman!

For extended close reading and insights, Neil Spencer, J. C. Gabel, and Tyson McVey. More who checked/discussed chunks of these words and ideas along the way—Dr. Jason King, J. D. Samson, Michael Patrick McDonald, Maxine Walters, and Webb Crawford. If I have misinterpreted, please send any brickbats my way.

All sorts of family supported me in every way imaginable, including Robert Katz; the Cherry-McVey clan, Cameron, Neneh, Naima, Tyson, Mabel; the Clennells, Bobby, Lindsey and Jake; Arlene "Bobby" Chung; Alexis Adler; Janette Beckman; Oberon and Scarlett Sinclair and Alex Schweder; Bill Wheeler; Dan Fox & Frieze; Alan Card; Nasser Ba; Aram and Dunia Best-Sinnreich;

Markus Detmer and Staubgold Records; RIP Mick Sawyer, my partner in Spellbound Pictures, producing/directing *Big World Cafe*, and Eric B & Rakim's *I Ain't No Joke* video. For my sterling editor Casey Kittrell, who is strong on both ideas and structure—and kindness and compassion. Thanks for working with me through life's twists. The University of Texas Press crew, Angelica Lopez-Torres, Robert Kimzey, and particularly Gianna Lamorte, who asked me to write this book after reading my brief piece in *Pitchfork*'s list of feminist punk songs—for which, thanks to the women of *Pitchfork* and the men who dig their ideas!

No way could I have planned it, but starting in Miami and ending in Ocho Rios, the writing of this book began and wrapped in friends' waterfront mansions—plus a little cottage in Oracabessa. For hosting and encouraging me, thanks to Ann and Colin Hodges-Smikle; the Trojan Records Jamaica crew of Jo Murray, Sly and Robbie, Wayne, Brian and Caroline Jobson, Barry "Bazza" Doughty, and Sshh and Zak Starkey; my most constant reader and sister in Chantage (our Afro-Euro duo), Eve Blouin; and my dynamic godchildren, Paloma and Olivier Parkes.

Writing this book was indeed a discovery, not least a reminder of the significance of sisters and sisterhood. Who knows who I would be without the Fictionaires, Jana Martin, Evelyn McDonnell, DJ Anita Sarko, writer/publisher Sue Steward (RIP), Eva Las Vegas (and August Darnell), Gina Birch and the Raincoats, Jeannette Lee, Geoff Travis, Janette Beckman, Neneh Cherry, Andrea Oliver, the Slits, the Delta 5, Chicks on Speed, Jill Cunniff and Luscious Jackson, Adriana Kaegi, Helen McCookerybook, Dunia (and Aram!) Best-Sinnreich and Jeni and Hollie Cook (and Paul!); and my artistic mentors, Moki Cherry, Caroline Coon, and Jayne Cortez. Extra hugs to Gina and Helen, for understanding and not freaking out when my original title happened to overlap with that of their ongoing documentary, *Stories from the She-Punks*. We live it, and thanks for understanding; you have started a genre!

Thanks always to my actual genetic sisters and their tribes, Susan in the middle and Big Sis Judy; I may have arranged their harmonies when we were little, but they still help to arrange my life.

Vivien Goldman, Jackson Heights, Queens, NY

INDEX

ABOUT THE AUTHOR

Born in London, Vivien Goldman has been a music journalist for more than forty years and was the trusted chronicler of Bob Marley and Fela Kuti. She was a member of the new-wave bands Chantage and The Flying Lizards; *Resolutionary*, a retrospective compilation album of her work, was released in 2016. She is an adjunct professor teaching Punk, Afrobeat, and Reggae at New York University, where the Vivien Goldman Punk and Reggae Collection is archived in the Fales Library. A former documentarian, her five previous books include *The Book of Exodus: The Making and Meaning of Bob Marley and the Wailers' Album of the Century*. Goldman co-wrote the book for *Cherchez La Femme*, the Kid Creole musical that premiered at the La Mama Theatre in NYC in 2016.